· Mother Lode sunset ·

The Mother Lode

A Pictorial Guide to California's Gold Rush Country

Photographs by Charles Moore
Text by Kristin Moore

Chronicle Books
San Francisco

Library of Congress
Cataloging in
Publication Data
Moore, Charles.
The Mother Lode.
Bibliography: p. 125.
Includes index.
1. California, Northern—
Description and travel—
Guide-books. 2. Historic
sites—California, Northern—
Guide-books. 3. California—
Gold discoveries.
I. Moore, Kristin. II. Title.
F867.5.M66   1983
917.94'0453   83-10113
ISBN 0-87701-247-4

Edited by Carey Charlesworth
Map illustrations on page 8
by Jim Moore

Acknowledgments
We'd like to express deep
gratitude to our friend Soren
Jensen of Chinese Camp. His
excellent command of heli-
copter flying allowed Charles
breathtaking opportunities
for aerials of the Mother
Lode Country. Soren's wide
experiences as a top-notch
freelance pilot (from Hollywood stunt flying to wilderness bridge building) made
our flying time most enjoy-
able. I'd also like to give
special thanks to my copy-
editor, Carey Charlesworth,
who miraculously managed
to condense my voluminous
script, derived from mountains of research, to a more
manageable size without
losing the essence of my
style and purpose. —*KM*

Chronicle Books
870 Market Street
San Francisco
California 94102

· Ladder and barn near Sonora ·

· Contents ·

Sunset from Jackass Hill over New Melones Dam

· Preface ·

*Y*ears before Charles and I met we had independently held dear the Mother Lode country. In February 1979, while still riding high from our honeymoon in Singapore, we decided to cure our jet lag by retreating to a quiet area for a few days. We chose Sonora as a base. There we rested and launched our leisurely explorations of the outlying vicinities. We had no immediate intention of leaving our San Francisco home and way of life, although we had thought of moving to a small town in two or three years. Within twenty-four hours, we had put a down payment on a house. Needless to say, the brief retreat more than paid off.

We've been falling more deeply in love with this entire area ever since we moved to Columbia in June 1979. To apply Charles's experience as an editorial and travel photographer to capturing the true romance of this historical country was an exciting idea.

And the work that grew out of it has enriched our lives. The same enrichment is available to one who reads this book, responds to the photographs, and takes a personal tour of the Mother Lode.

When you visit these small towns walk the back streets, study the artifacts and gold mining relics, and visit the local hangouts to meet the old-timers. Their stories are so vivid, and sometimes so preposterous, you'll find it difficult to wind things up when it's time to move on.

In this book we cover some of the small details that convey the colorfulness of the Mother Lode as well as historical events that have played an important part in building California, affecting the lives of people from all over the world. By taking you on a photographic tour of the gold country, we silhouette today's romantic Mother Lode against glimpses of her full and glorious past.

· Mother Lode Round-up Parade in Sonora ·

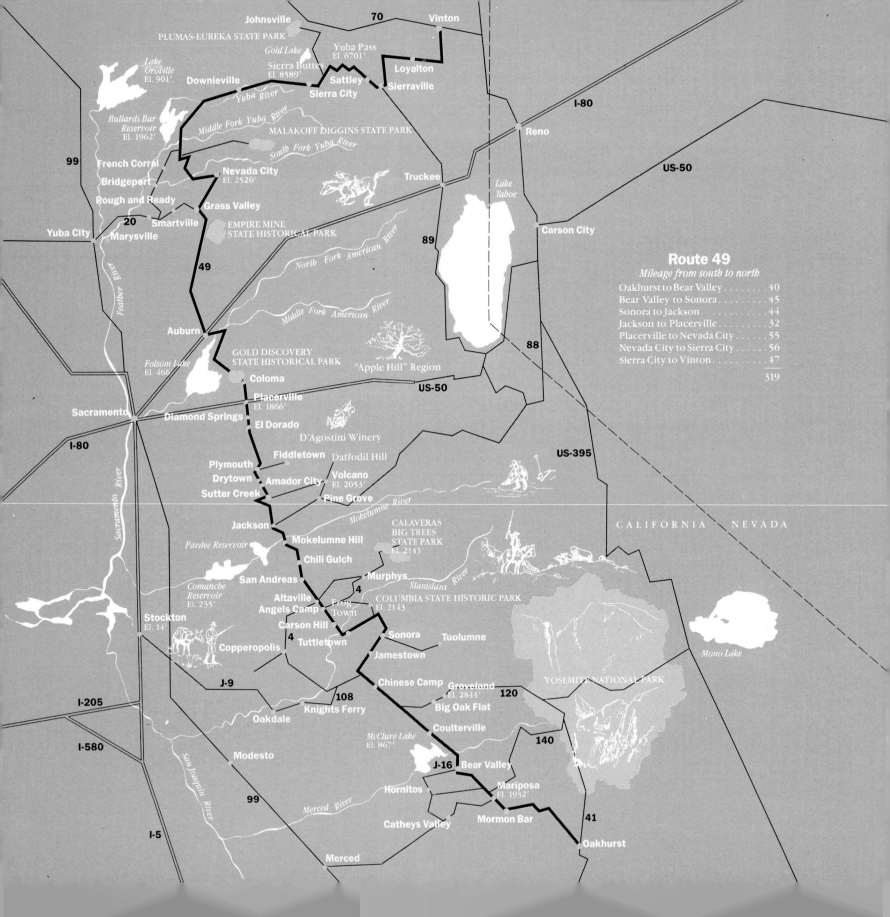

Johnsville

PLUMAS-EUREKA STATE PARK

70

Vinton

Gold Lake

Yuba Pass
El. 6701'

Loyalton

Lake Oroville
El. 901'

Downieville

Sierra Buttes
El. 8589'

Sattley

Sierraville

I-80

Yuba River

Sierra City

Bullards Bar
Reservoir
El. 1962'

Middle Fork Yuba River

MALAKOFF DIGGINS STATE PARK

South Fork Yuba River

Reno

99

French Corral

Nevada City
El. 2520'

Truckee

US-50

Bridgeport

Rough and Ready

Grass Valley

Lake
Tahoe

20

Smartville

EMPIRE MINE
STATE HISTORICAL PARK

89

Carson City

Yuba City

Marysville

North Fork American River

49

Middle Fork American River

88

Auburn

GOLD DISCOVERY
STATE HISTORICAL PARK

Folsom Lake
El. 466'

"Apple Hill" Region

Route 49
Mileage from south to north

Oakhurst to Bear Valley	40
Bear Valley to Sonora	45
Sonora to Jackson	44
Jackson to Placerville	32
Placerville to Nevada City	55
Nevada City to Sierra City	56
Sierra City to Vinton	47
	319

Coloma

Placerville
El. 1866'

US-50

Sacramento

Diamond Springs

El Dorado

I-80

D'Agostini Winery

US-395

Plymouth

Fiddletown

Daffodil Hill

Drytown

Volcano
El. 2053'

Amador City

Sutter Creek

Pine Grove

Mokelumne River

Jackson

CALAVERAS
BIG TREES
STATE PARK
El. 2143'

CALIFORNIA   NEVADA

Pardee Reservoir

Mokelumne Hill

Chili Gulch

Murphys

Stanislaus River

San Andreas

Comanche
Reservoir
El. 235'

Altaville

4

COLUMBIA STATE HISTORIC PARK
El. 2143'

Angels Camp

Frog Town

Mono Lake

Stockton
El. 14'

Carson Hill

4

Sonora

Tuolumne

Tuttletown

Copperopolis

Jamestown

J-9

Chinese Camp

Groveland
El. 2844'

120

YOSEMITE NATIONAL PARK

I-205

108

Knights Ferry

Big Oak Flat

Oakdale

Coulterville

140

I-580

McClure Lake
El. 867'

J-16

Bear Valley

Modesto

Hornitos

Mariposa
El. 1932'

99

Merced River

Catheys Valley

Mormon Bar

41

I-5

Oakhurst

Merced

Sacramento River

Feather River

San Joaquin River

· Invitation to the Tour ·

The term *Mother Lode* was coined to describe primarily one rich vein of California's gold. It extends from Melones, near Sonora, in the south nearly to Auburn in the north. Today the Mother Lode and, at its feet and head, the Southern Mines and Northern Mines areas are traversed by Highway 49 and crisscrossed by scenic backroads, and they are still as rich for the leisurely traveler as they once were for the gold-seeking argonauts.

The Southern Mines area was the wildest West of them all. Here, in the years after gold's discovery in 1849, Joaquin Murieta wove his legend. Lynchings were most common in this section, where warfare broke out between the recently defined "Americans" and "foreigners" and also where the Chinese waged tong wars. This is where the tour north along Highway 49 begins.

The Mother Lode was the geographic center of the gold rush, and it is plentifully scattered with miner's marks. Hundreds of gold camps are now nothing but ghost towns not even marked on modern-day maps. The only signs left of these once-frenzied camps are abandoned mine tunnels, coyote holes, the piles of waste rock called tailings, and remnants of Chinese rock walls. Today in the Mother Lode, sleepy Western towns dot a landscape of rolling, grassy foothills sprinkled with fine old oaks and pines. Search out the rustic backroads in this middle country, and make side trips to the smaller forks and creeks of the big rivers. You won't have to look far to find a picnic spot offering peace and privacy.

Just north of Nevada City, Highway 49 turns east and climbs through the spectacular high Sierra. At this far end of the Gold Country, reaching an elevation of sixty-seven hundred feet, the Sierra Buttes tower over many glacier lakes and vast forests that offer superb high-country recreations. Ruggedness and serenity are the backdrop for the Northern Mines gold towns, nestled in pines along rushing rivers. Johnsville marks the end of the tour and the northernmost point of the whole 270-mile stretch, which these days is termed inclusively the Mother Lode.

Even according to Hinton R. Helper, a miner who was unsuccessful and who in 1855 published a book warning of the California "delusion," the gold rush territory rates superlatives. He wrote,

I will say, that I have seen purer liquors, better segars, finer tobacco, truer guns and pistols, larger dirks and bowie-knives, and prettier courtesans here, than in any other place I have ever visited; and it is my unbiased opinion that California can and does furnish the best bad things that are obtainable in America.

The sights and places to eat and stay recommended in these chapters are intended as guideposts—some of the best things California can furnish today. Because chambers of commerce can help with particular requirements in your travels, addresses of the offices to contact in the Gold Country are listed at the back of the book. A list of inns—recommended favorites—also appears there. Be sure not to miss exploring on your own.

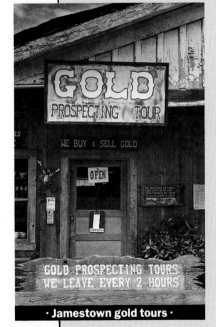

· Jamestown gold tours ·

· Mother Lode landscape along Highway 49 near Drytown ·

The Mother Lode

Butterflies and Bear Pits

1

· Oak tree at sunset ·

MARIPOSA TO SONORA

MARIPOSA, THE HEART OF THE ORIGINAL MOTHER LODE, IS NOW the Gold Country's southern gateway. Once called Logtown, the town's name is Spanish for butterfly, and several species are common here. Take a walk through Mariposa. Quite a few historical sites remain, including the oldest courthouse in continuous operation in California, serving the people since 1854. Be sure to go upstairs and see the courtroom chambers with the potbellied stove and handsome wooden, pew-type benches. It's an outstandingly proud building, displaying a large English clock tower. Mariposa's History Center is one of the most impressive museums in the Mother Lode. The way its artifacts are displayed is the remedy for the coldness of standard unadorned museum cases housed in rooms of institutional green that discourage visitors from lingering. This special project, put together by Muriel Neavin, is a real showplace, including a fully furnished Gagliardo dry goods store, moved to new quarters but set up exactly as it was in the late 1800s. Here in the foyer of the History Center are items on the store's shelves more than a hundred years old but brand new from the basement storage (where the unpopular, slow-moving goods were kept). Among the displayed goods are stiffly starched dress shirts, high button shoes, and many kinds of kitchen gadgets. Next move through to the Daulton Room.

Recreated here are such additional well-appointed visual delights as a one-room miner's cabin, a sheriff's office, and a wealthy lady's dressing room.

After you view the considerable number of display items inside, touring the grounds around the History Center will keep you busy for at least another hour. You'll find a great blacksmith's shop and gold mining equipment of every shape and kind, from a fully restored and operable five-stamp mill to a well-preserved arrastra—a crude, drag-stone pulverizing mill. There are even Miwok Indian dwellings and a sauna here. According to local lore, the Indians would build a fire to heat stones in the center of the wooden-roofed underground sauna. Then they would cover the entrance with a deer hide, throw water on the rocks, work up a good sweat, and follow with a bath in a nearby cold stream, which got rid of all human odor. One purpose of this regimen was to enable the hunters to get close to the deer.

Several picturesque side roads connect Mariposa to Hornitos and Bear Valley. A drive on Catheys Valley or Indian Gulch Road in the spring leads past lovely flowers, creeks, and peaceful rural landscape. As an alternative route out of Mariposa take Highway 49 north from Mariposa to Bear Valley, then follow J16 west eleven miles to Hornitos. Within a few yards of one another near these roads are purple and white lupine, yellow monkeyflowers, purple mariposa lilies, red paintbrush, Western pennyroyal, white popcorn flower, buttercups, Sierra thistle, golden yarrow, fairy lanterns, and both orange and white poppies.

· Vault door at the Mariposa History Center ·

The now-sleepy village of Hornitos was started in 1850 by outcast Mexicans from nearby Quartzburg, where the whites had gained predominance. With a population growing to nearly fifteen thousand, Hornitos became one of the richest and toughest of the early-day mining camps. It had a multiracial society composed of Germans, French, Italians and English, as well as Mexicans, Chileanos, and other Spanish-speaking people, plus Chinese, who worked as twenty-five-cents-per-day laborers, and black slaves brought by Southerners.

Hornitos has the strongest claim to famed bandit Joaquin Murieta, who apparently had a hideout here with his many friends. Becalmed now, this small town of fewer than a hundred people still holds a lot of interest. Hornitos is one of those sites where

· Miwok tepees of cedar bark ·

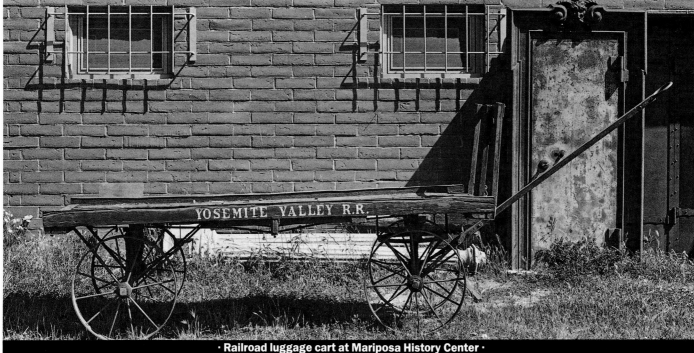

· Railroad luggage cart at Mariposa History Center ·

one's sense of history is much stronger than in some more extensive, if restored, gold towns. Here, see the ruins of the Ghirardelli chocolate empire's first building, erected in 1858. The ghostly quiet surrounding these crumbling walls, the mere shell of a once-bustling merchant's headquarters, provoke the imagination. An abundance of huge old rosebushes in town add beauty and fragrance in summer and spring.

The old jail is charming, with a little bit of cactus growing near the front-

· California poppy ·

· Gold-mining power generator at Mariposa History Center ·

· The Bandit Joaquin ·

The gold rush brought out both the good guys and the bad guys and, as still happens, it was the bad guys who got most of the press. Probably the most highly publicized yet misrepresented of the latter group was Joaquin Murieta, the so-called Robin Hood of the Mexicans.

Fictional stories say that witnessing his brother's lynching and the ravishing of his sweetheart, Ana Benitiz, triggered Joaquin's two-month rampage, but there exists no real evidence of these incidents or even proof that he had a brother. Conversely, terrible deeds were attributed to him that could not physically have been accomplished by one bandit, not even with a jet-powered horse.

In 1851 Joaquin Murieta stole twenty-nine horses from a Mexican rancher. He was caught and whipped for the crime. Records from the newspapers claim he committed twenty-four and possibly twenty-nine murders. Joaquin was an excellent horseman (always stealing his fresh mounts) and a deadeye behind the trigger. He relished close calls, even daring to rob and murder in plain view of a pursuing posse and somehow escaping like a genie. He attacked Chinese and Anglos equally. Usually he victimized unarmed men, which accounts for the large number of his Chinese victims—the Chinese generally were peaceful and few owned firearms.

At the height of the publicity Joaquin Murieta was reported to be thirty-five years old and to have a band of well-organized guerrillas. The most likely attempts at truth are that he was only nineteen years old and merely seized opportunities spontaneously, riding with fewer than a handful of men.

Joaquin Murieta did nothing to earn his Robin Hood reputation, but there could have been a number of Mexicans named Joaquin who contributed to it. Certainly the Mexicans were given reason to turn to violence; when the "Americanos" took over, the Mexicans were run out of their own homeland and off their mine claims and property. Later they were charged a foreign miner's tax, and many were unjustly accused and subsequently punished for all sorts of crimes, including murder. At one point miners passed resolutions calling on all Americans to "exterminate the Mexican race from the country." As the *San Joaquin Republican* asserted, "If an American meets a Mexican, he takes his horse, his arms and bids him leave."

The man who finally ended Joaquin's wild spree was a bounty hunter named Harry Love. Called the Black Knight of the Placers, he had a reputation for letting his prisoners escape so he could shoot them in the back—a sport he apparently enjoyed.

Consistent with all the other discrepancies in the Joaquin Murieta legend, it is not even known whether the head that Harry Love brought back as proof for the reward money was Joaquin's. Accounts by people who paid to see it on exhibit said the hair was too light and curly and the eyes were blue—hardly the black-haired, brown-eyed Mexican of earlier descriptions. Perhaps, after hearing about his own death, Joaquin Murieta hightailed it to Mexico and lived happily ever after.

· Hornitos, a favorite hideout ·

door stoop giving it a Mexican flair. There's a small museum of artifacts inside set up by the E Clampus Vitus Society, an early men's service organization of sorts, familiarly known as the Clampers. Typical of the members' humor, the Latin motto above the door means "I believe because it is absurd."

To find the grave markers shaped like little ovens—*hornitos*—that gave the town its name, wander through the cemetery of St. Catherine's Catholic Church. What's unknown about these grave markers is whether they were built by Indians to be used as ovens or are copies of ovens made by Mexicans for their grave coverings. A pitiful-looking iron cross is said to be the oldest landmark in the area. It leans out of a loose mound of stones covering a grave site that suggests the hasty work of the gold rush days, when people had less time to bury their dead and more important things to do. The late-nineteenth-century to early-twentieth-century gravestones tell the town's story, from the many infant deaths to the varied nationalities.

Nearby, back on Highway 49, is Bear Valley, a small, quiet town full of history, though little of history's imprint is visible. Bear Valley was the headquarters of Col. John C. Frémont, who in 1847 purchased a floating Mexican grant of forty-four thousand acres for three thousand dollars. After gold was discovered he floated his grant to include the Mother Lode all the way from Mariposa to the Merced River. He grubstaked experienced Mexican, Cornish, and Welsh miners to work his placers, and in 1859 he

· Sheepherder near Chinese Camp ·

· Filming an explosion in a reconstructed tent town ·

· The Clampers ·

The E Clampus Vitus Society, a group of hard-drinking, fun-loving men, has in its fanciful way made quite a contribution to California history. The first chapter of this secret lodge, founded in 1850 by J.H. Zumwalt, met at the St. Charles Hotel in Sierra City.

What drew the Clampers together was poking fun at all the other fraternal organizations. However, the members had a charitable side, dedicating themselves to the betterment of life for "widders and orphans—especially widders." When they were not partying they anonymously gave food to the needy and helped deserving children with their education.

Revived in the 1930s, the E Clampus Vitus Society is constituted in chapters each headed by a Noble Grand Humbug and each maintaining a meeting place termed the Hall of Comparative Ovations. The members still meet in full unregalia, cut up, and have a good time.

· **A Clampers Hall of Comparative Ovations in North Bloomfield** ·

was netting more than a hundred thousand dollars per year with two stamp mills operating. Later, in 1863, he sold his grant for six million dollars.

From the size of Bear Valley you wouldn't even expect to find a public eating place there, but up the street across from the ruins of Frémont's store is the gourmet Bon Ton Cafe. Established as a saloon in 1860, the blue and white Bon Ton Cafe is now a culinary showpiece owned and operated by Nicole and Steve Bischoff. The excellent weekend brunches fea-

· Hornitos' oldest relic ·

· St. Catherine's Catholic Church at Hornitos, built in 1862 ·

· 1862 covered bridge in Knights Ferry ·

· Restored firehouse in Knights Ferry ·

ture homemade beer bread and jam, Russian blintzes, and eggs benedict, all the dishes accompanied with fresh fruit. The dinner menu varies with such nightly specials as Indonesian satay, veal piccata, linguini with clams, and curried chicken. Ruins of an old 1857 dry goods store next door to the Bon Ton building serves as a pleasant outdoor dining patio in summer.

Seventeen miles northwest of Bear Valley on Highway 49 is the town of Coulterville, which is named for George W. Coulter, a storekeeper and

inn proprietor early in the town's history. Coulterville was a tent town called Banderita, in reference to the little flag Coulter flew over his store. They say Coulter's hotel was the first in the town and that its water was pumped by the power of two Newfoundland dogs.

There's a handsome locomotive steam engine parked under Coulterville's hanging tree. It's a reminder of what was the only railroad in Mariposa County, on a short and winding route. The majority of the gold taken

out of this area was run through stamp mills that were steam powered and wood fueled.

Coulterville today is a mere shadow of the busy town in its prime, when it had twenty-five saloons and as many as ten hotels. It has been the victim of fire on three occasions; the final blaze, in 1899, destroyed nearly the entire town.

The sights to see in Coulterville include the Jeffrey Hotel, made of Mexican bricks of clay and rock. Its Magnolia Room is a real "Gunsmoke"-

· Jamestown's Sierra Railroad at water-tank movie location ·

type saloon, featuring memorabilia. Another favorite spot is the Sun Sun Wo Company Store, at the end of Main Street in what was formerly a Chinatown of significant size. This 1851 adobe structure was established and run as a general store by Chinese merchants, and it remained a general store until 1920. Some of its ranch customers, far away yet dependent on the store's supplies, had direct telephone lines hooked up to it. Today the old store is in remarkable condition, displaying snacks, souvenirs, and antiques. Proprietor Danny Moyers is happy to answer questions about its past.

Appropriately called Chinese Camp, the town about sixteen miles north on Highway 49 formerly had a Chinese population exceeding Coulterville's. It was founded in 1849 by Cantonese from Hong Kong after they struck rich claims and then were run off by white miners. They found gold again only a mile from their original site, and they named their new settlement Chinese Camp. In time more than five thousand Asians settled here. In

· Jamestown's Main Street ·

· The Diversity of Settlers ·

The massive settlement of the Mother Lode in 1849 included adventurers of many races and nationalities. The following account was taken from a letter by a traveler from Ohio written when he visited a placer mining town. He saw there, he said, a sign advertising a French restaurant. Being hungry, he entered to discover an establishment run by a mulatto from Louisiana who rented the premises from a Jew and employed a Chinese cook and a young Austrian waiter. Being served there the same evening were a Scotsman, an Irishman, and a Welshman, and in the meals they had the meat had been purveyed by a Dutch butcher, the vegetables by an Italian gardener, the bread by a French baker, the milk by a Portuguese milkman, and the restaurant's laundry was done by a Mexican woman.

The considerable diversity of cultures remaining in the Gold Country is manifested in myriad details. For example in some locales you can determine the nationalities of the early residents by the local vegetation. The Mexicans planted cactus around their settlements, the Italians planted vineyards (you'll notice wild grapevines in the central Mother Lode), and the Chinese planted the ailanthus trees—"trees of heaven"—at their camps.

· Homesteader/prospector with faithful companion ·

1856 the non-Chinese numbered approximately one thousand.

Chinese Camp was the site of the first tong wars between the Sam Yap and Yan Wo Tongs. The wars are traceable to tong members' move to save face when a large boulder was rolled from one camp over the boundaries of the other. Although more than two thousand people battled with handmade axes, spears, and a few guns, only four died.

The town's starkly beautiful St. Francis Xavier Catholic Church was built at the peak of the hill in 1855. The setting for this church and its old cemetary, among oak trees and the fragrant narcissus that bloom wild in the spring, is perfectly restful.

Walk around Chinese Camp; there are barnyard animals, lots of rosebushes, and a great grocery store and bar owned and run by John and Dottie O'Brien. The O'Briens are as colorful as the paraphernalia behind their bar. With great enthusiasm they assist in casting for the movies periodically made here. At times they also act in the films themselves. Get acquainted with the locals at the bar, and listen to a few yarns.

A seventeen-mile side trip west off Highway 49 on Highway 108 leads to Knight's Ferry, which was settled in 1843 by William Knight. Though a fur trader and a mountain man, he made his living here ferrying gold seekers across the Stanislaus River. In 1854 a covered bridge replaced Knight's ferry services, but by then his name had stuck.

At the end of town are the gristmill ruins and the New England–style cov-

· A familiar landmark of the Mother Lode country ·

· Calf roping at Sonora's Mother Lode Round-up ·

ered bridge that replaced the ferry service. Several old homes around the town also stand in beautiful settings along the river. The most unusual historical structure here is the jail cell built entirely of iron on solid rock near the covered bridge. Don't miss the 1871 Hook and Ladder Company No. 1 on the main street, which is attractively restored. Inside is its old cart, with the ladders and leather buckets intact.

Back on Highway 49 and eight miles north is Jamestown, fondly called Jimtown by the locals. Jimtown was founded by Col. George James, a San Francisco lawyer whose name was honored after he treated the entire camp to free champagne. Despite a devastating fire in 1966, Jimtown has done an excellent job of preserving the old gold-rush-days appearance of the main street. Some great old buildings house attractive gift shops, antique stores, and fine old hotels. The Hotel Willow, Jamestown Hotel, and National Hotel all have handsome dining rooms for romantic meals. For a change of pace try a bucket of steamed clams at the Mountain Steamer Pizza Parlour, or, for fine Mexican food, any of the specialties at The Smoke are highly recommended.

Jimtown's proudest claim to fame is the glorious Sierra Railroad in Railtown 1897, where steam locomotives blow black clouds of billowing smoke and whistle shrilly. Many people have seen those trains in the movies filmed here, such as *The Virginian, High Noon, The Great Race,* and *Shadow Riders,* as well as several western television series. Check with the depot to see

· Gayland "Mutt" Mutzner, a local Sonoran ·

· Doc Monte, magician ·

· Baby blue eyes and visitor ·

· Spring monkeyflowers along meandering stream near Jamestown ·

which excursions are running. Equally fascinating are the shop complex and the round house where these historic beasts are serviced.

Just four more miles up Highway 49 is Sonora. This town was called the Queen of the Southern Mines, and it was once the largest and busiest city in the southern region. Originally, in 1848, Sonora was founded as two parts—Campo Sonorense and Campo Americano. The Americans who moved here after California became a state charged the "foreigners" a twenty-dollar-per-month tax, which drove the Mexicans to separate grounds. Repealing the tax some time later did not neutralize the animosity it had engendered.

During its heyday Sonora had the reputation of being a rowdy town, holding fights that pitted bears against horses. Perhaps also for sheer entertainment, fist fighting and gang brawling on downtown Washington Street were everyday occurrences.

Sonora today is the Tuolumne County seat and has a lot of pride in her past. Washington Street, as busy a thoroughfare as ever, is lined with historical buildings that house shops and services of all kinds. Sonora gets a lot of tourism year round because it is on major routes to popular ski resorts, Yosemite National Park, and Stanislaus National Forest.

The most photographed building in this southern end of the Mother Lode is probably Sonora's famous St. James Episcopal Church, known simply as "the red church." Built in 1860, this pretty building stands at the west end of Washington Street. A matching red building across from it on the left is

· **Sonora's famous red church in winter** ·

· "Old Ben" Fullingham, veteran prospector ·

the 1896 Street-Morgan Mansion, once the home of lumber tycoon S.S. Bradford. This house is one of the most elaborately embellished Victorians in the entire Mother Lode. On Bradford Street off Washington, the Tuolumne County Historical Society, housed in the old 1857 jail, has an excellent museum of gold rush memorabilia, including period costumes, old letters, and diaries. Take the time to drive or walk the residential areas. The Victorians are grand.

The "good food" coffee shop here, called the Cafe Europa, is open twenty-four hours a day. You can't beat the homemade pies or the prices. It's practically an institution. Sonora also has fine accommodations, at the historic Gunn House and Sonora Inn.

Strolling through town, you'll notice a creek that runs under a section of Washington Street. This is Woods Creek, which used to flood frequently during the heavy winters. On February 8, 1857, during a storm a local citizen spied a six-pound nugget lodged in an eddy near the old Wells Fargo building's stoop. He came away twelve hundred dollars richer. This was one of many occasions when the rain-swollen river brought unexpected riches to passersby. Today you can still see an occasional prospector panning here. ■

Bucket Brigades and Angel Wings

2

· Shadows of the past ·

**COLUMBIA STATE
HISTORIC PARK
AND
MOANING CAVERN**

COLUMBIA, ANOTHER THREE MILES UP HIGHWAY 49 JUST NORTHWEST OF Sonora is a must on your gold towns tour. Since 1945 this uniquely representative Gold Country town has been a state park, the only preserved gold town in the United States. After a visit to Columbia you will know what the gold towns looked like; it deserves its title, the "Gem of the Southern Mines." On March 27, 1850, Dr. Thaddeus Hildreth and his brother George found gold here while working with a few other prospectors and, as with other rich finds, the word spread fast. In a few weeks "Hildreth's Diggins" was a tent-town home for several thousand gold seekers. About 130 years ago Hildreth's Diggins, later to be named American Camp and finally the more dignified Columbia, was the richest, wildest, and largest mining town in the world. At one time it housed more than fifteen thousand residents, who dug up, washed out of the earth, and labored for $87 million worth of gold. Of that gold, $55 million worth was weighed on the beautiful scales still housed in the old Wells Fargo office. In its heyday, the town boasted more than 150 places of business, including some 21 produce stores, 30 saloons and restaurants, 17 dry goods stores, 12 hotels, 9 fruit and confectionary shops, 8 carpenters, 7 bankers, 5 doctors, 5 law offices, 4 Mexican fandango dance halls, 4 liveries, 3 blacksmiths, 2 wagonmakers, and

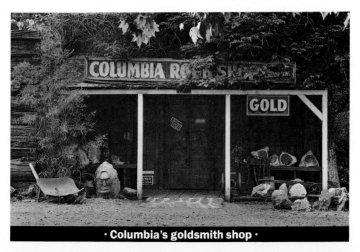

· Columbia's goldsmith shop ·

· Main Street in Columbia ·

a brewery. Of course there were also express offices and boot, liquor, drug, and tobacco stores, plus the laundry, barber, and photo shops.

Many reminders of the expensive taste this rich little town once afforded are still on view, such as the ornate black iron railings imported from Europe to use on upper-story balconies. And the elegant and garishly decorated hand-pump fire engine named Papeete is a true example of the rich residents' extravagant tastes. It was as if they believed the gold would never run out.

For entertainment (when circumstances were on the upswing), live shows were given at the Fallon House, featuring such greats as Lola Montez, and circuses with elephants and lions were brought to town. July Fourth was always celebrated in a big way, as it is today. There was also an arena for bloody bull and bear fights; despite the town's history of abundant riches spend on fine imported goods, great sums went for wickedness as well.

Quite a few Chinese lived in Columbia during the gold rush, and the Anglos grew jealous of their success. In 1852, after the anti-Chinese Foreign Miners Tax (like the anti-Mexican tax) was repealed, a mass meeting turned into a vigilante movement forbidding the Chinese to mine gold in Columbia. But the Chinese continued to settle, and among their businesses were opium dens and houses of prostitution, which increased the already prejudiced town's ire. When the 1857 fire destroyed the Chinatown area, white townsfolk seized the opportunity to ban the Chinese permanently. Much debasing treatment drove one Chinese

· Al Ponce, a native Columbian and part-time actor ·

· **Kelly Noteman and friend, a Columbia doll** ·

· **Alvira Mahoney, State Park docent** ·

to shoot it out with the local sheriff. (Neither is reported to have died.) It was the only gunfight involving a Chinese ever recorded.

As in other gold rush towns, Columbia's fires were devastating. The first one, in 1854, destroyed practically the entire town, which had been constructed mainly of wood. The 1857 fire too destroyed everything that was wood framed, plus several of the newly built brick buildings. The town was rebuilt again, using ever more brick as well as the iron window and door shutters that were a standard protective device in the Mother Lode. And in 1859 the citizens' volunteer fire department bought Papeete. Being prettier than she was adequate for any large fires, she was joined by a bigger engine, the Monumental, in 1860.

After years of hydraulic mining, which implacably laid waste to the land around Columbia, the supply of gold diminished. Finally what remained was far too difficult to obtain and, as happened with other gold towns, Columbia was nearly abandoned. The boom-town population dwindled to little more than five hundred people.

Today the original town of Columbia is the center of Columbia State Historic Park and is the best example remaining anywhere of what a real gold town was like. In the interests of maintaining the historic appearance, Main Street is off limits to cars. This makes getting acquainted with the antique town a lot easier and more fitting.

In Columbia you can sip sarsaparilla or beer in one of the saloons, watch a

· When Women Went West ·

At the beginning of the gold rush a few "proper" ladies made the difficult journey west. When one did come to town she brought out the best in the men.

Among the recorded recollections of George Napoleon, who was himself a miner, is an account by his friend J.D. Peter of when the first woman set foot in Columbia.

Everybody quit work; there were six or eight thousand of 'em. They built decorated arches over the street and marched four miles down the road with a band of music to meet her and escort her back to camp. By the time they got back, the town was jammed full of miners that had come from miles around to get a glimpse of the woman.

Once women were an established presence, a number went into business. They could make a killing as cooks, or nurses, or by taking in washing at exorbitant rates. Many made more money than their hardworking husbands away at the diggins. One industrious woman was purported to have earned eighteen thousand dollars selling pies she baked over an open campfire.

These were, of course, all traditional pursuits. Columbia goes a step farther with a story hinging on a schoolmarm's honor. Evidently one of Columbia's madams, "Big Annie," was accused of pushing the teacher into the street. The chivalrous boys of the fire department got so angry they dragged their pump over to Annie's place of business and proceeded to turn the high-pressure hose on it—washing her right out of the house. She forthwith left town.

· **Summer Bartholomew, actress in period dress** ·

· An old wooden water wheel ·

· Rock formation detail ·

melodrama at the Fandango Theater, listen to a banjo and washtub at the state's oldest barbershop, watch the blacksmith at work, or taste old-fashioned, hand-dipped chocolates at the Candy Kitchen. The list goes on—visit a working custom carpenter shop, old-time tintype photo studio, leather shop, newspaper shop (for the *Columbia Gazette*), dry goods store, and general mercantile store. There are also some inactive but authentically renovated shops, such as the apothecary store, Chinese herb shop and altar, butcher shop, ice house, livery stable, and Wells Fargo office with its huge, handsome gold scales. For the exciting stagecoach rides buy tickets at the old stage depot next to the bank. The stagecoach runs several times a day during the summer and usually on weekends off season.

You'll find an old miner's cabin at one end of the main street full of typical 1850s furnishings—bleak but practical. Columbia also has a Masonic Hall and buildings of the I.O.O.F. and The Native Sons of the Golden West as well as a wonderful old school. To get to the school, walk or drive up Pacific off Main Street and turn up School-house Street. This 1860 building on Kennebec Hill was in use until 1937. It displays old wooden desks, old books, wood-burning stoves, organs for choir classes, and all kinds of antique classroom paraphernalia.

Columbia's museum has the best display of real gold you'll find, showing it in its varying forms, nuggets and dust and quartz. The museum also has a model illustrating the difficult process of restoring the old buildings, and a free slide show several times

· Miner's cabin and hydraulicked boulders in the State Park ·

· Clyde Ratliff, a guide at the Hidden Treasure Mine ·

· Papeete ·

When Columbia was feeling its richest, nothing exemplified the extravagance of its tastes better than the acquisition of Papeete. It was 1859, two years after the town's second major fire, when the citizens of Columbia selected a committee to go to San Francisco and purchase a fire truck. What the committee found was a hand pumper built in Boston in 1852. After being embellished for the ownership of the king of the Society Islands (of whose island Tahiti Papeete was the capital city), the little machine had been sailed to San Francisco's harbor and abruptly abandoned. The ship's crew was one of many whose members left their posts to go to the gold fields. When the committee laid eyes on Papeete it was love at first sight, and money was not an issue. If it was good enough for a king then it definitely was the right one for Columbia, and the citizens took it home.

Columbia still owns Papeete. The truck still does the town proud, too, when it takes first prize at the annual Fireman's Muster for its unparalleled pumping abilities.

· Papeete in action at Columbia's annual Fireman's Muster ·

daily depicts Columbia and the gold rush days.

Wander among the weirdly shaped gargantuan granite boulders around Columbia to witness the effects of hydraulic mining. Then, to see hard-rock mining, take the thrilling tour through the Hidden Treasure Mine with Matelot Gulch Mining Company guide Clyde Ratliff. This takes you through more than seven hundred feet of mining tunnels in what is still a working mine. There's no better way to learn exactly what mining is all about. Ask for Clyde at the old mining shack across the street from the Wells Fargo building. You can also take gold panning lessons there (with the guarantee that you'll get some color) and, if you get the fever, even buy the proper supplies.

Columbia has some wonderful restaurants. Particularly notable and within the park is the City Hotel, which in addition to being an elegant inn has a restaurant with a reputation for fine French food. The dinner menu proceeds through escargots and vichyssoise to roast duck á l'orange and lemon soufflé. The champagne brunches and gourmet lunches are equally pleasing. And the variety of fine dishes, all made entirely from fresh ingredients, is surpassed only by the selection of wines—particularly California wines from small, family-operated premium vineyards. One reason for the City Hotel's excellence is its association with nearby Columbia Community College's Hospitality Management Program. Reservations are recommended.

At one time the Fallon House Theater drew crowds of miners for perfor-

· Greased pole climber ·

· Peter Griggs, Master of Ceremonies ·

· Fireman's Muster hand cart race ·

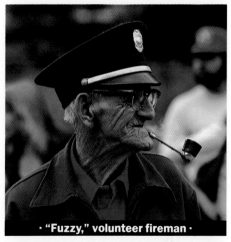
· "Fuzzy," volunteer fireman ·

· Ryan Scheller on July Fourth ·

· Stagecoach driver taking a break ·

mances by the likes of Lola Montez, Lotta Crabtree, and Edwin Booth. The theater was built in 1857 and is still in use. Performances are given in summer; some day they may be year round.

July Fourth in Columbia is a celebration of Americana. There is an energetic parade with homemade floats and costumes, followed by pie-eating, sack-racing, fence-painting, and greased-pole-climbing contests, while square dancers and musicians perform in the streets. And there is a lot of food—from watermelon slices to corn on the cob.

The biggest and most famous event in Columbia is the annual Fireman's Muster, held the first weekend in May. Members of volunteer fire departments come from all over California, dressed in period uniform and riding in their antique, spit-polished red fire engines trimmed in sparkling brass. Men and women compete in bucket brigades and hose-cart races, and the men highlight competition by putting the old-time hand-pump engines through their paces. Many other events are also scheduled in Columbia, including craft fairs, wine tastings, air shows, and antique auto rallies. (Consult the Tuolumne County Chamber of Commerce for dates.)

Before leaving Columbia drive out Parrotts Ferry Road to tour Moaning Cavern. The forty-five-minute tour is quite an eye opener, especially if you like caves; this one is listed as California's largest cavern. The gold miners, whose "early" exploration of this cave began in 1851, were long preceded by prehistoric man. More than thirteen thousand years ago natives and wild animals accidentally fell

· Bill Davis and Patrick Clark, barbershop duo ·

· Kelly Noteman and Laurice Wright at July Fourth parade ·

· Columbia Gazette and Eagle Cotage ·

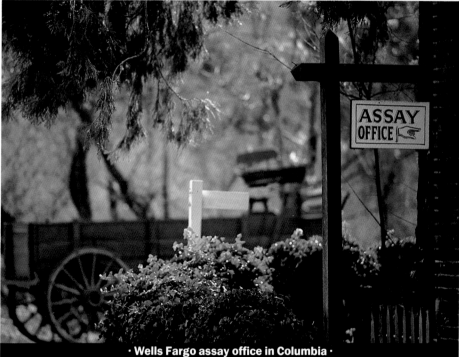

· Wells Fargo assay office in Columbia ·

through the original small surface opening, tumbling down 165 feet to die on the main floor. You'll see the evidence on display. Today an iron-guarded spiral staircase provides a secure way to the bottom of the cavern. The formations are beautiful, inspiring names as fanciful as Igloo, Angel Wings, and King Kong.

For the truly adventurous spelunker, Cave City Expeditions offers a rugged five-hour tour through huge caverns with deep lakes and gorgeous crystal formations. Experienced guides outfit

· Fossilized quartz ·

· Moaning Cavern formations ·

you properly and take you crawling, rope climbing, and rafting through an unforgettable cavern system. (Ask for more information at the Moaning Cavern office or write to Cave City Expeditions, P.O. Box 78, Vallecito, California 95251.)

Once at Moaning Cavern you're almost in Vallecito. From there, you may want to take the Highway 4 side trip described in the next chapter. Otherwise, return to Highway 49 and head north towards Tuttletown.

· Supply store at Matelot Gulch ·

· Iron door of Columbia jail ·

· **Private home in Columbia State Park** ·

· **Old Columbia Engine company firehouse** ·

· How They Mined the Gold ·

The earliest way to find gold in the Mother Lode was to turn over rocks in a riverbed and pluck out the nuggets. In some places gold really was that plentiful. Even the first serious method used by the argonauts required only a strong back, lots of patience, and a wide-rimmed shallow pan or a wicker Indian basket. With such a pan the miners washed riverbed soil in water, using rotating motions to progressively discard dirt, which was relatively light; the heavier placer gold settled to the bottom. "Placer" refers both to the glacial deposits that carry gold and to the forms of above-ground mining that tap these deposits by means of water.

From panning the miners graduated to rockers and cradles, long toms, and sluice boxes. The rocker and cradle worked on the same principle as the pan but enabled the miners to process more pay dirt faster. The wooden long toms were boxes about twelve feet long and ten inches deep. One end, wider than the other, received the water carrying the dirt and conveyed it to a perforated metal screen that allowed the finer suspended particles to be sifted into an attached box.

To operate each of these methods the miner needed a continuous flow of water, which explains why so many mining ditches and canals were constructed. Today these same ditches are used throughout the Mother Lode by utility companies.

A sluice box was a bigger, more elaborate version of the long tom, sometimes fifty to a hundred feet in length, enabling miners to channel an entire river through their equipment. To shovel, sort, and wash required a team of several men. Later, flumes and dams were constructed to divert water to new courses and thereby expose riverbeds for mining. Making these diversions was very hard work, requiring many hands. And often the rainy-season floods wrecked the fruits of the painful labors within hours.

In 1853, when gold became more difficult to find in the riverbeds, the miners invented the hydraulic method. They used incredibly long rawhide hoses and giant monitor nozzles weighing up to a ton apiece to blast streams of water on the earth at high pressure and so expose more of the placer gravel. The gravel then fell into sluice boxes. The water came from flume and canal systems hundreds of miles long that carried melted snow from large dams high up in the mountains; a five-inch nozzle conveying water from a four-hundred-square-foot reservoir shot out more than eleven thousand gallons per minute.

Such huge operations did major damage to the surrounding countryside and wildlife. The valley streams were backed up, which caused flooding, and vast quantities of "slickens" (runoff mud) ruined precious farmland. This destructive method wasn't abandoned until 1884, when it was legally banned by Judge Lorenzo Sawyer.

Malakoff Diggins State Park has an awesome example of the effects of "hydraulicking." Another area heavily mined by this method is at Columbia, where giant, oddly shaped rocks have been left exposed around the town and its outskirts.

In the 1890s miners began dredging, using huge gas-engine-powered machines to bring up riverbed gravel from deep holes. Remnants of the piles of discarded gravel, called tailings, can still be seen along riverbanks throughout the Mother Lode.

Another placer mining method is called drift mining. This mode

· Gold-mining tools of the trade ·

tapped ancient stream-beds where gold ore was deposited under rock formed from lava flows, earthquakes, and landslides. Tunnels called adits were drilled to reach the gold-bearing gravel and bring it to the surface. This method is being used today in such areas as Table Mountain—a volcanically formed, mesa-like mountain several miles long in the Jamestown area of Tuolumne County.

Early miners believed that all gold originated in streams, like the gold first discovered in the Mother Lode. They didn't realize at first that gold also lay in solid rock beneath the surface of the ground. When they discovered gold-bearing quartz outcroppings, the whole picture of mining changed. Solid mountains were blasted away with ordinary gun powder. (Dynamite wasn't invented until 1860.) And deep inside shafts in the earth miners worked with pick and

shovel, bringing the rock up to the surface in ore carts pulled by mules. Mining gold from the solid quartz rock was called, naturally enough, hard-rock mining.

When the quartz rock had been knocked free it was crushed so the gold could be separated from it. One mechanism for crushing the rock was the Mexican arrastra, a circular area of flat rock enclosed by a low rock wall. Heavy boulders called drag stones were attached by chains to poles which were attached to a center

revolving post. The ore was placed in the path of the circle, and when the stones were dragged around by mules or other beasts of burden, the ore was crushed, as in a giant mortar.

The most economical and advanced method of crushing ore was the stamp mill, which crushed the rock under the weight of heavy giant stamps that moved up and down like pistons. Some mills had as many as a hundred stamps, crushing the quartz to a fine powder or slime. After the crushing the gold was separated out through

an amalgamation process, by running it over mercury-coated plates. The mercury that attracted the gold was heated to 2,600°F, a process that released the gold and vaporized the mercury (to be recycled). The gold was then melted and poured into molds. The resulting ingots weighed eighty-nine pounds. Thus, if the scenarios in Westerns were true, when the gold stolen from stagecoaches was packed eight to ten bars to a horse for a quick getaway the poor horse wouldn't have been able to budge.

A number of fine old stamp mills are on display throughout the Gold Country. Of course, most of the remnant mining equipment is inoperable, having been abandoned when the rush was over. Yet, many geologists estimate that to date no more than 8 to 15 percent of the gold has been removed from the quartz mountains of the Mother Lode.

· Columbia movie extras at the blacksmith shop ·

· John O'Brien, actor and casting agent ·

· Movie extra on Main Street ·

· The Newington boys, local extras ·

· Filming *The Shadow Riders* with Sam Elliot on Main Street ·

· Local character actors on location ·

· Fishing the New Melones Reservoir ·

Jumping Frogs and Daffodils

· Springtime romance ·

TUTTLETOWN TO SUTTER CREEK

S*O LITTLE IS LEFT OF TUTTLETOWN, IT'S EASY TO MISS. BRET HARTE CLERKED* there at Swerer's Store (now in ruins), and Mark Twain was one of the store's regular customers. Not far away up a well-marked side road is an authentic replica of Mark Twain's cabin, last rebuilt in 1922. The chimney evidently survived the original cabin's fire and was used again in the restoration. This was the cabin of the Gillis brothers, Jim and Bill, who had Twain as a guest for five months in 1864/65 while he was busy writing his famous tale "The Celebrated Jumping Frog of Calaveras County." The location of the cabin is a place called Jackass Hill. Some of the families that live there are related one way or another to the Gillis brothers. Why was it named Jackass Hill? It started out as a stopover on the trail to Melones and Tuttletown, offering overnight grazing for the pack mules and burros. The nighttime braying of sometimes two hundred animals at once earned the title. The hill is said to be literally laced with shafts and tunnels from quartz mining. Back on Highway 49 you'll pass some attractive ruins on the left edge of the highway, made of brick and stone. This was the James Romaggi House, built in 1852. At one time several buildings lined this stretch of road, all part of the settlement of Albany Flat. Romaggi was a proud farmer who put his energies into orchards and vineyards instead of prospecting. Browse the

· Reflections at Mark Twain's cabin ·

· Oak trees with mistletoe ·

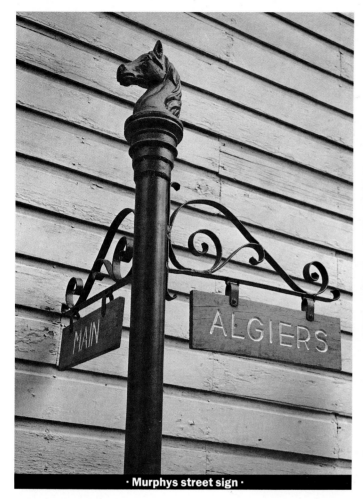

· Murphys street sign ·

· Antique store in Murphys ·

curious exterior; this ruin tells its own stories.

Just before entering the main section of Angels Camp, you will meet an intersection with Highway 4, on which you can take a side trip to see Vallecito, Murphys, and Mercer Caves.

Vallecito is five miles east of Highway 49 on the way to Murphys. There's not much remaining of the original town, once a rich Mexican mining camp, founded in 1850. As with many of the formerly wealthy small gold towns, one of the buildings surviving the rigors of time is the Wells Fargo office. Also standing is the old 1851 Dinkelspiel Store next door. L. Dinkelspiel was the first agent to work for Wells Fargo & Company in Vallecito.

It's not far to Murphys, definitely on anyone's list of favorite Mother Lode towns. Settled in 1848 by John and Daniel Murphy while they were looking for gold, the town was originally known as Murphys Rich Diggins. Its residents claimed for it the title "Queen of the Sierra," and their placer claims outperformed any in Calaveras County. They kept their Wells Fargo office busy, shipping $15,444,000 in gold from the 1850s to the 1860s.

This pleasant, well-preserved town conveys the sense that time stood still after the gold rush days. The main street is lined with large locust trees and elms, shading many century-old stone buildings. The biggest attraction is the Murphys Hotel and Lodge, known in 1856 as the Sperry and Perry Hotel. It was considered the finest hotel outside San Francisco.

· Pie-eating contest from *Seven Brides for Seven Brothers* ·

· Dapper Dandies barbershop quartet at Murphys Octoberfest ·

· Filming *Seven Brides* in Murphys ·

The Presidential Suite was even furnished with a grand piano. Built to take care of the steady increase in visitors going to see the then recently discovered Big Trees of Calaveras, the Murphys Hotel had some notable guests. Be sure to look at the listing of the famous on the old hotel register, including Mark Twain, U.S. Grant, and Horatio Alger. Even Black Bart stayed here, under another of his aliases—Charles Bolton. (His real name was Charles Boles.)

Hollywood is fond of Murphys as a good-looking Western town for locations. Peruse Main Street and you'll agree. Among many structures worth viewing here is the 1856 Peter Traver Building, housing the Old Timers Museum. Don't miss the E Clampus Vitus Wall of Comparative Ovations just outside.

One favored place to eat (or, rather, indulge) is the Peppermint Stick Ice Cream Parlour, a "slow paced, high quality family food establishment." This old-time shop has the best assortment of homemade candies and ice cream desserts you can imagine. Sandwiches are offered, too, and they make filling lunches, but most patrons can't keep away from the ice cream sundaes.

The Murphys Hotel has a fine restaurant, for elegant dining at lunch or dinner. Spend some time in its great Western bar, where many prize game heads watch from behind the bartender.

Just outside Murphys, only one mile north on Sheep Ranch Road, is Mercer Caves. You'll see the turnoff clearly marked on the main street in

· Wild daisy field near Angels Camp ·

· Lee Hinman and Pac-Frog ·

· Detail of sheer rock wall along Highway 49 ·

· Mariposa lily ·

Murphys. At one time this cave was called Calaveras Caverns; Calaveras means skulls in Spanish, and that's what was found when the caves were first discovered. The bones of a woman and her two children are believed to be the result of the Miwok burial practice of lowering bodies into caves. This network of caves is entirely different from Moaning Cavern, because the caves were formed not by underground water but from a fissure created by an earthquake millions of years ago. Among the formations is the highly unusual aragonite, a

· Round-up time near Angels Camp ·

fragile frostlike crystal. Specimens of aragonite brought the Mercer Caves international recognition by winning a Grand Prize at the 1900 World's Fair in Paris. The caverns have been open to the public for nearly a hundred years. The climb through the eight distinctive chambers involves lots of stairs but also many view and rest stops, and the tour is well worth the forty-five minute walk and inexpensive fee.

On to Angels Camp. Either retrace your route along Highway 4 all the way to Highway 49, or, better yet, take the scenic Murphys Grade Road just west of Murphys. It'll drop you right into town. Founded by George and Henry Angel in 1848, Angels Camp began as a simple trading post. By accidentally firing his muzzle loader while cleaning it one day, a miner named Bennegar Rasberry exposed a chunk of gold-filled quartz. The town grew by leaps and bounds in no time, and before long Mark Twain made it and himself famous. The contest in "The Celebrated Jumping Frog of Calaveras County" has been an official event of the town since 1928.

At the Jumping Frog Jubilee, held the third weekend in May, you'll see not only lots of people having a real good time but also some serious sport. Both humor and anxiety prevail; don't try to touch anyone's lucky champion frog until after the $1,500 first prize is awarded.

Angels Camp has another of those relatively unspoiled main streets with lots of neat shops and great gold rush architecture. The museum at the north end

· **Antique store in San Andreas** ·

of town is worth a stop for the old steam engines, the elegant 1880s hearse, and the impressive rock collection.

If you're in the mood for good food try the Sierra Club, where you can choose from a good American menu, which includes homemade pies, classic hamburgers, and thick milkshakes.

Six miles up Highway 49 is Altaville. It was named Forks in the Road in 1852, after that was called Winterton, and later still was known as Cherokee Flat before it became Altaville. The most

· The Knoys in rendezvous regalia ·

· "Grizzly" at Mountain Ranch's Mountain Men Rendezvous ·

· Alias Black Bart ·

Charles Boles, also known as Charles Bolton, was a dashing gentleman, poet, and long-distance walker who also happened to be an accomplished robber. Under the alias Black Bart he committed twenty-eight robberies between 1877 and 1883, but he is remembered equally for his love of the finer things. It was highway robbery that supported his taste; successful gold mining simply eluded him. Black Bart often walked thirty miles a day, always arriving at the scenes of his crimes on foot. For his work he donned a long coat and wore a flour-sack hood with eye holes. Typically his method of operation was to stand in front of the lead horse of an express stage as it rounded a slow corner; staying out of firing range, he would then simply order the driver to "Please throw down your box!" And he would break the strong box open with a hatchet. It's rumored he never fired his gun and possibly never even loaded it. His commanding presence was what made those tough stagecoach drivers obey.

The following poem is one he wrote and left at the scene of one of his hold-ups:

Here I lay me down to sleep
to wait the coming morrow.
Perhaps success, perhaps
defeat
and everlasting sorrow.
I've labored hard and long
for bread
for honor and for riches.

But on my corns too long
you've tred
you fine haired sons of
bitches.
Let come what will, I'll try
it on
my condition can't be
worse
and if there's money in
that box
'tis munney in my purse.

During a holdup near Copperopolis, Black Bart was wounded slightly and he dropped a handkerchief that bore a laundry mark. A special agent by the name of Harry Morse traced the mark and eventually was introduced to a finely dressed, polite-mannered man. To Morses's—and San Francisco's—surprise, this outstanding citizen, who was well liked and was known to all under the name Charles E. Bolton, turned out to be Black Bart. He confessed only to the last robbery, and he served four years in San Quentin, where he signed in as T.Z. Spaulding. After his release Black Bart was never heard from again.

· Blacksmith Paul Osborn with Black Bart—style shotgun ·

· Panning for gold on Angels Creek ·

historic structure left in town is California's oldest continuously operating iron foundry, working since 1854 when J.M. Wooster started it. And the old two-story stone Price and Garibardi Store is still in fine shape.

The next main stop is San Andreas, eleven miles north on 49, but before heading in that direction consider a side trip to Copperopolis. This site of rich copper mines is on Highway 4 eleven miles east of Angels Camp. It still has a lot of charm and several old buildings.

· Mokelumne River near flood level ·

San Andreas is the Calaveras County seat and, compared with a town like Murphys, it's a bustling metropolis. You have to look a little harder here to find the few remaining historical buildings. The courthouse where legendary Black Bart stood trial is still here, and he served some time in the jail cell behind it. The courthouse is now the home of an outstanding county museum and the local chamber of commerce.

In stark contrast to San Andreas's city atmosphere and only eight miles north is the popular getaway town of Mokelumne Hill, known widely as Mok Hill. The Western flavor of this town makes a real strong statement the minute you drive in. Founded in 1848, Mok Hill became one of the biggest and richest of the Mother Lode mining camps. It was the site of two "wars." One was between miners over a Chilean doctor accused of using slave labor to work his claims; the other started when several French miners raised their national flag over a rich discovery and, in an obvious excuse to jump their claim, a group of Old Glory faithfuls tried to drive them out of their camp.

· Victorian house in Jackson ·

Mok Hill's Hotel Leger is a popular retreat. On weekends you'll often see people lounging on the porches, unwinding with a few friends over beer. The hotel's restaurant serves excellent meals, and next door is an active playhouse.

A short seven miles farther is Jackson. To do this town justice takes some time. First it was called Botilleas, a Spanish word for bottles. The namesake bottles were frequently left in the stage stopover's nearby freshwater spring. Later the town was named after the famous old Indian fighter Col. Alden Jackson. Jackson used to be a rollicking, rambunctious town, and it didn't close the last of its bordellos until the 1950s, when Sacramento's politicians were cleaning up California's image.

Although placer gold was found at Jackson, the real riches came after hard-rock mining began in the quartz lodes. The Kennedy and Argonaut mines yielded more than $140 million in gold before they were closed in 1942. Some shafts extended down fifty-eight hundred feet, the deepest in the United States.

The Kennedy Tailing Wheels just outside Jackson Gate are an awesome sight. Standing more than sixty-eight feet high, the four wheels were built in 1912 to lift the tailings of a 100-stamp mill over two hills to an impounding dam. The giant wheels were water powered, utilizing gravity feed supplied by high, long flumes. Until you see it in real life you can't imagine the genius and labor this operation required.

Jackson has handsome Victorians and historical architecture throughout. A particularly photogenic structure is the St. Sava's Serbian Orthodox Church, which was erected in 1894. It's the mother church of this sect in North America.

The National Hotel's Louisiana House bar is a great place to hear some honky-tonk piano, and on an energetic Saturday night you can sing along with the locals plus visitors from all over. For dining, The Balcony restaurant is recommended. With impeccable service, a romantic atmo-

· Wall ruins of James Romaggi House, built in 1852 ·

· St. Sava's Serbian Orthodox Church in Jackson ·

· Court Street Inn, Jackson ·

sphere, and superb continental cuisine, this cozy place rates high.

If you enjoy the quiet comfort of bed and breakfast inns look up Jackson's Court Street Inn. It is the only inn in this part of the Mother Lode in the National Register of Historic Places, and it is also designated a state histor- ical point of interest. The inn is an elaborately restored 1870s home, with antique-filled rooms that are ele- gant right down to the fresh flowers. After your reservation is made (chances are mighty slim of getting a

· I.O.O.F. Building in Mokelumne Hill ·

· Old doorway with hollyhock in Volcano ·

· Kennedy tailing wheel in Jackson ·

· Decaying wagon wheels at Daffodil Hill ·

room at the last minute on a weekend) your biggest decision will be which of the seven entirely different rooms to choose. Wine is offered in the sitting room each evening, and the morning's full breakfast is delicious. A stay at the Court Street Inn also offers the opportunity to meet Mildred Burns, one of the Mother Lode's nicest innkeepers.

A side trip extending fifteen miles from Jackson offers two attractions. The eventual goal is Volcano, a town that could win any contest for most character concentrated in two blocks. On the way to Volcano is Chaw-Se Grinding Rock State Park, the only park in California's state system focusing mainly on Indian culture. To reach the park and the town take Highway 88 east to Pine Grove; then follow the Pine Grove–Volcano Road.

Chaw-Se allows a glimpse into the past. In this ancient territory of the Miwok you can enter bark teepees and ceremonial roundhouses. Several of the oldest and largest valley oak trees in California are here, and in the middle of this setting is the famous seventy-seven-hundred-square-foot grinding rock with its nearly twelve hundred mortar holes and many hieroglyphics.

The park's museum offers thorough displays and audiovisual programs, prepared by Miwok who have first-hand knowledge of how their ancestors lived and how their people live today. If you go there in September, time your visit to see the Acorn Festival, in which the Miwok perform tribal dances and play games in celebration of the annual acorn harvest just as their ancestors did every fall before them. Chaw-Se is sure to

increase your appreciation of the pre-gold-rush era.

Volcano, called Soldier's Gulch when it was founded in 1848, today is one of the most genuine, noncommercial gold towns left. It's a photographer's delight. And, not only rich in gold, this little camp is historically rich in culture. Volcano had the first rental library in California in 1854, called the Miner's Library Association. There was an admission fee of a dollar with monthly dues of twenty-five cents. The idea of the community "little theater" was born here when the Volcano Thespian Society organized in 1854. The town lays claim also to the state's first literary and debating society, and just two miles away California's first observatory was built—on Observatory Hill. The name Volcano stems from the mistaken notion that

· The Indian Inhabitants ·

At one time California had a native population of more than a hundred thousand, including the Culumah, Maidu, and Miwok tribes of what became the Mother Lode. The Culumah Indians lived in the valley through which the Coloma Road now runs, near the Maidu, who lived in what today are the Coloma and Nevada City areas. The Indians were said to know the loca-tions of all the gold-bearing quartz in the region. They used the outcroppings to make stone points, for war or hunting; mortars, for grinding; and chipped knives, for carving meats, building dwell-ings, and dressing skins. They also used the quartz for decorative and ceremonial pur-poses. However the gold itself, which had no practical use in daily life, carried no real value.

Of all the tribes, the Miwok are the most introverted and peace-ful. Their roots extend deep in California, with their ancestors present as early as 2000 B.C. In the 1770s their territory in the area of the Mother Lode was primarily from Mariposa in the south to El Dorado County in the north.

Depending on where they lived, the Miwok's basic diet consisted of acorns, fish, grasshop-pers, such game birds as quail, ducks, geese, and pigeons, plus jackrab-bits, gray squirrels, ante-lope, and deer. They cooked their foods and even boiled water in their tightly woven bas-kets, by putting hot stones in them. Many Mother Lode museums contain fine examples of these handsome baskets.

Miwok dress was made from deerskin and furs. The men often wore flowers in their hair. The tribes lived an unre-stricted lifestyle as basic food gatherers, without planting or harvesting or herding any livestock.

A common (and deroga-tory) nickname for these tribes, who dug bulbs and tuberous plants for food, was "the diggers."

Eventually, when white men invaded for the gold and stayed to oc-cupy the land, the Indians who could not adapt were either killed or confined to reserva-tions. By 1910 the Miwok, mercilessly exploited, were reduced to a mere seven hun-dred people.

One of the reasons the white man treated the Miwok so brutally, not unlike animals, was the preconditioning of the "overlanders." Many of the emigrants from the East had terrible, dehu-manizing experiences at the hands of more fero-cious tribes during treks across the plains. For the warfare instigated there the peace-loving Miwok, too, paid the price. The repercussions of the exploitation are still felt today. In spite of them, the proud Miwok are struggling to pre-serve their heritage and religion.

· "Swift Turttle," Miwok Jonathan LeDeaux ·

the hollow it was built in was at one time a volcanic crater.

One side of the main street has striking stone ruins that are continuously decaying and crumbling to the ground. The most notable and photographed ruin in town, which was the first assay office in Volcano, finally fell down in 1981. It will be rebuilt to house the Volcano Community Theater so as to seat more people for the popular summertime melodramas and other plays.

The three-story, 1862 St. George Hotel is, like the Hotel Leger, a popular weekend spot, with a family-style dining room and nice accommodations. As you wander through town you'll find several boutiques. A fine rock shop is in the old Sing Kee Store at the end of the main street. Nearby you'll see the cannon "Old Abe," used during the Civil War to keep gold from the hands of Confederate sympathizers. (It was never fired—the Union partisans had no cannon balls.)

A real highlight of a visit to Volcano is brunching at the Jug and Rose. Brunch is all the sourdough pancakes you can eat, with hot spiced syrup, scrambled eggs, ham, a fresh fruit compote, and a beverage. Marvelous lunches also are served. The sandwiches are made with homemade bread and accompanied by a fresh fruit garnish. All of the selections are presented with such style and attention to detail that they're as pleasing to the eye as they are to the palate. On a hot summer day try one of the blackberry milkshakes decorated with fresh flowers and mint leaves.

If you're in the area in late March or April be sure to take the three-mile

· Volcano's Main Street adorned for the Christmas season ·

· Daffodil Hill's "Blue Boy" peacock ·

side trip on Sutter Creek–Volcano Road to Daffodil Hill. The McLaughlin family has planted nearly three hundred name varieties of bulbs over the years, crowding the hill with more than two hundred thousand fragrant blossoms of daffodils, narcissus, tulips, hyacinths, crocuses, and more. And if you're lucky the family peacocks might strut their stuff for you.

To reach Sutter Creek and return to Highway 49 continue along scenic Sutter Creek–Volcano Road about eleven miles. In spring you'll see an array of colorful wildflowers all along the route.

John Sutter was bitterly disappointed at the loss of all his mill workers to the newly discovered gold diggins. For his next pursuit, he set out with some hundred Indians in his employ to try his own luck at gold prospecting, and he arrived at the site of Sutter Creek in 1848. Once again, however, he failed to find his fortune. Legend has it he liked the bars and ladies too much.

A much happier story is Leland Stanford's. Rather than sell his shares of

· **Exotic tulip at Daffodil Hill** ·

· **Daffodil Hill springtime** ·

· Stone ruins ·

· Old jailhouse in Murphys ·

· Lichen-covered gate ·

the not-too-lucrative Sutter Creek Lincoln Mine for five thousand dollars, he waited, the claim yielded considerably more gold, and he eventually sold his shares for four hundred thousand dollars. That bonanza launched him. In the career that followed, Stanford succeeded as railroad magnate, governor, senator, and of course founder of Stanford University.

At Sutter Creek, plan to spend a good deal of time browsing through the intriguing gift and antique shops. The well-preserved main street has lots of old buildings, including the 1894 Levaggis Opera House, the 1859 Brignole General Store, and the 1859 I.O.O.F./Masonic Hall. Knight's Foundry is rare for being a water-powered operation. It has been pouring molten metal for stamp-mill parts since 1873.

If you intend to stay in this vicinity first try the Sutter Creek Inn. Once you've looked at the comfortable but wonderfully unusual suites you'll want to spend a special weekend here. For a savory family-style Italian dinner try the Bellotti Inn. Established in 1860, the restaurant's decor is grand, and the veal scallopini is delicious. Or for a simple but tasty snack go to the Pasty Place and have an old-fashioned Cornish dish. Both of these restaurants are on the main street. ■■■■

· The Hale Ranch near Daffodil Hill ·

Vintage Wines and Apple Pie

AMADOR CITY

TO

AUBURN

· Firehouse in Drytown ·

*T*HE NEXT GOLD TOWN IS AMADOR CITY, THREE MILES NORTH OF SUTTER Creek. It was named for the Indian fighter Jose Maria Amador, from the San Ramon Valley. The main street has several century-old buildings, and the overall appearance, compared with that of other Mother Lode towns, is quaint. As you enter town you'll pass the old wooden Schaffer's Diggins, now the home of John's Gallery. Not only is the outside of the store picturesque, with old wagon wheels and antiques on the porch, inside are some of the finest handcrafts and gifts you'll find. John and Sandy Jurisich left city life to establish John's Gallery, which has baskets, rugs, handcarved wooden kitchen utensils, handmade soaps, candles, and jewelry. Farther up the street are many fine shops, with plentiful antiques and good food. Say hello to Maria and Jack Baker at the Buffalo Chips Emporium. In a late-1800s building they serve great breakfasts, lunches, and ice cream desserts. If you want to stay in Amador try the lovely Mine House Inn, once the Keystone Mine headquarters. Just up the road on Highway 49 is Drytown. Dating from 1848, it's the oldest town in the country. It was named after the usually bone-dry creek, not for any scarcity of saloons, which, as a matter of fact, once numbered twenty-six. Even though much was lost in an 1857 fire, there are several old buildings to see here. The post office, which is also a candle and thrift shop, has an old marble floor originating when the store was a butcher shop.

The big attraction in Drytown is the Piper Playhouse, which presents melodramas on Saturday nights in the summer. Join in with the hissing, booing, and cheering while you're entertained by the Claypiper Players.

You'll reach Plymouth just a couple of miles north of Drytown. It started in 1870 as a mining town, but not much is left to see from those days. The foremost gold rush building still intact is the old Empire Building on Main Street, headquarters of the once-rich Consolidated Mines. Plymouth is now a farming town, particularly in walnuts, grapes, pears, and sheep. It is also home of the Amador County Fairgrounds, which has an attractive display of reconstructed Western shops. And Plymouth's fairgrounds have recently been used as the site for Fiddletown's annual Fiddlin' Contest because of that small town's high turnout of participants and audience in the last few years. Fiddletown was bursting at the seams trying to accommodate in one day almost five thousand lovers of good country music.

On a spring or summer side trip to Fiddletown, a few miles east of Plymouth on Fiddletown Road, you'll see lots of wild sweet peas. You certainly won't miss the giant fiddle perched on top of the community center next to the firehouse. The town was named by Missourian settlers who were said to "mine when it was wet and fiddle when it was not." When the creeks ran dry from lack of rainfall they couldn't wash the pay-dirt, and the dry times and fiddlin' around were plenty.

At one time Fiddletown had the largest population of Chinese outside San Francisco. There's a unique rammed-earth-constructed combination Chinese home and herb store. A Dr. Chew Kee took over from a Dr. Yee and ran the herb store until it finally became the home of bachelor Chow Fong You, called Jimmy Chow, until he died in 1965 at age eighty-five. Open now only on special occasions, it remains just as it was left, complete with private Chinese altar.

Once you've reached Fiddletown, the famous D'Agostini Winery is only three miles farther on Shenandoah Road. Its tasting room is worth the jog north.

When you've returned to Highway 49 and are heading north toward Placerville, you'll drive through the peaceful small towns of El Dorado and Diamond Springs. In early times both were freight stops on the Carson Emigrant Trail. Diamond Springs was at one time a rich town. It was founded in 1849; today, however, the only gold-rush-era structures still intact in this peaceful town are the 1852 I.O.O.F. building and the 1857 Louis Le Petit building.

It's said that when gold was still plentiful chickens were persistent gatherers of small nuggets. At Diamond Springs, in 1856, one was killed for a Sunday dinner and the gizzard panned out $12.80

El Dorado, incorporated in 1855, was formerly called Mud Springs. The old 1858 Wells Fargo building has a great restaurant named Poor Reds. The food is outstanding Western barbeque, cooked in a genuine wood pit, and the colorful bar has earned a reputation for its drinks. Poor Reds claims to be the originator of the golden cadillac—a fizz-type after-dinner drink made of Galliano, white creme de cacao, and fresh cream.

The next major stop is Placerville. For a period ending in 1854 it was known as Hangtown for its vigilante activity.

Placerville owes its success not to gold but to its role as a strategic communications and transportation crossroads. This was the first service-oriented stop west of the Sierra for the many brave crossers of the Overland Trail. The town acquired the first telegraph in the West in 1853, and later it was a major Pony Express stop. Further income for the town was derived from the stream of people passing through on their way to the silver Comstock Lode in Nevada.

Many famous people had their beginnings in Placerville, including Mark Hopkins, who ran a grocery store; Philip Armour (the meat king), who sold food to miners; and John Studebaker, who made wheelbarrows here during the gold rush. U.S. Grant kept all the saloons in business while he was stationed in Placerville.

The Placerville man who filled the bill of California's motto—"bring me men to match my mountains"—was "Snowshoe" Thompson. From 1856, at age twenty-nine, to 1876, at almost fifty, he delivered medicine, supplies, and mail across the Sierra between Placerville and Nevada. Thompson held true to the U.S. Postal Service promise to deliver in all weather con-

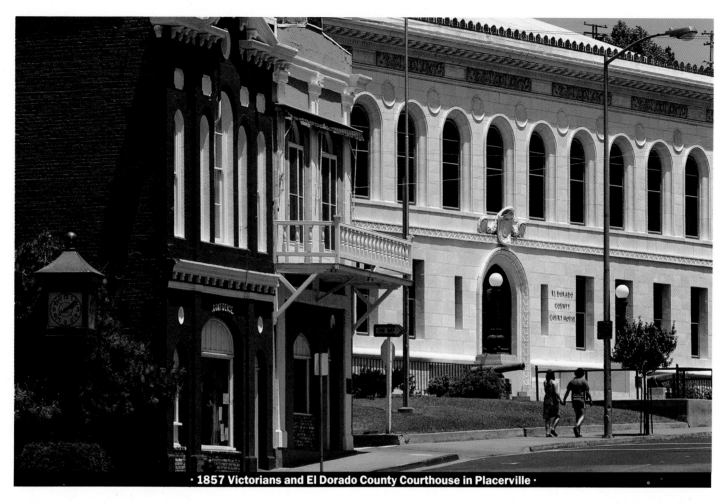

· **1857 Victorians and El Dorado County Courthouse in Placerville** ·

ditions by traversing the deep snows on nine-foot wooden skis. The normal weight of his load was sixty to eighty pounds, and on each trip it took him three days to go into Nevada, then two days to return. In twenty years, he never failed to get through.

Placerville has a lot of history to see and some tasty local products. Aside from the city hall on the main street and the old bawdy house next door, both built in 1857, the sights to seek out are in the Gold Bug Mine at Bedford Park. Its tunnel is one of only

two in the entire Mother Lode open to the public for a close-up look. You can walk into a well-lighted, 420-foot tunnel with plenty of head room and immediately be swept back a hundred years. The surrounding Bedford Park has a pretty creek, and it's a perfect picnic spot.

Ask the local chamber of commerce on Main Street for a map of the Apple Hill area. The pleasant drive there leads through orchards and Christmas tree farms. Many of the local growers sell their goods directly, along with

apple pie, spiced cider, apple butter, and even apple doughnuts.

Next is Coloma, where the gold rush madness began. As California's first boom town Coloma grew from two thousand mill workers in 1848 to ten thousand in 1849.

A windy but scenic seven-mile drive north of Placerville drops you into the beautiful, 220-acre Marshall Gold Discovery Historic State Park. Approximately 70 percent of Coloma is part of the park, which has a partic-

· **Rammed-earth Chinese herb store in Fiddletown** ·

· **Fiddletown's famous landmark** ·

ularly serene atmosphere, encouraging you to wander about. In the spring pentstemon, poppies, sweet peas, and blackberry bushes bloom throughout the grounds. The lush picnic areas offer many tables under shady oak trees.

The main attraction for most visitors at the park is the full-size replica of Sutter's Mill. If you arrive on a weekend you'll have a chance to watch it operate. The park has so many things to see, from mining methods to stage coaches, that it's best to start at the

museum and get a detailed guide to help you identify and find them all. The museum is first rate, with both exhibits and film presentations. Look into the old "Mormon Cabin" opposite the mill and the miner's cabin, showing the 1850s lifestyle. It's like peering into the past.

On the hill behind Coloma is a larger-than-life statue of James Marshall, pointing to the site where on January 24, 1848, he discovered gold on the American River below. This monument, where he lies buried, is only a

short walk from Marshall's cabin, the 1859 St. John's Catholic Church, and the 1856 Emmanuel Episcopal.

If you're an art lover, visit the Friday House (circa 1855). This was the home and gallery of the late California artist George Mathis, who depicted the Gold Country in pen, ink, and color. His family still runs the gallery and sells beautiful lithographs in the shop.

On the edge of town is the Sierra Nevada House III, a popular restaurant, soda parlor, and hotel. The beau-

· Winetasting in the Mother Lode ·

Winetasting in the Sierra foothills has become a favored way to tour the territory. The Mother Lode is California's oldest wine country. Wineries were abundant in the region in the late 1800s, but most were closed during Prohibition and the decline of gold mining. Now a reawakening is taking place. Since the 1970s Amador County's fabulous zinfandels have been redeveloped, and throughout the foothills experimentation with other premium varietals has been extremely successful.

The most historic of the current cellars is the D'Agostini Winery, situated eight miles east of Plymouth on Shenandoah Road. It has been in operation since 1856, and the original wine cellar is still in use. This state historic landmark offers some fine tastings in a setting rich in history and winemaking experience.

The other wineries in the Mother Lode (most established since 1973) are primarily family-owned operations that produce exceptional wines. Among them are Kenworthy Vineyards and Montevina, near the D'Agostini Winery; Stevenot Vineyards, east of Jackson up Sheep Ranch Road; and El Dorado Vineyards, east of Placerville off Highway 50.

For a printed guide to several of the Mother Lode's finest wineries, write to Sierra Foothill Wineries, P.O. Box 438, Somerset, California 95684.

· Grapes at harvest time ·

· **White-water rafting** ·

tiful Vineyard House, rumored to be haunted, is a fine dining spot and Victorian-style inn. It's highly recommended. The lavish saloon downstairs in the cool, rock-walled basement has a surprisingly warm atmosphere.

Up the hill past the Vineyard House, north approximately one mile, is the ghost town of Gold Hill. It is a special attraction to Japanese visitors, who come to see the lovely garden shrine near the Gold Hill School. The shrine was erected in remembrance of the United States' first Japanese settle-

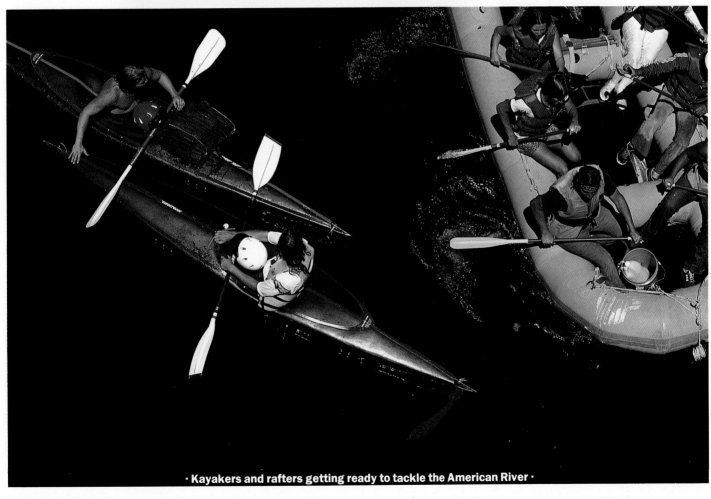

· **Kayakers and rafters getting ready to tackle the American River** ·

· Covered wagon and mule resting on way to Placerville ·

· **James Marshall's cabin at Marshall Gold Discovery Historic State Park** ·

ment. In the late 1860s the Wakamatsu Tea and Silk colony brought here thousands of mulberry trees, tea seeds, grape cuttings, and bamboo roots in hopes of starting large-scale tea and silk operations. Although the crops were not markedly successful, the Japanese greatly influenced California's farming methods.

There's not a lot left to see at the old settlement of Pilot Hill, but what is still there is one of a kind—the Gold Country's only plantation-style mansion. Eight miles north of Coloma on Highway 49 are the sad remains of "Bayley's Folly." This 1862 Louisiana-style roadhouse was built by Alcandor A. Bayley in anticipation of those who would need accommodations while traveling nearby on the proposed Central Pacific Railroad. The railroad, however, was rerouted to pass several miles away, and the Bayley House railroad hotel never realized its potential.

To guide a party led by the explorer John C. Frémont from the Sacramento Valley to the Sierra, fires were burned on the highest hill near the town. Thus the "pilot" fires of the town's name.

A few miles beyond, at Cool (once a limestone diggins), turn east from Highway 49 onto Highway 193 to have a look at Georgetown. Early on this town was called Growlersburg, because the nuggets were so large they were said to growl in the pans. The side trip is worth the extra time for more than the showy display of summer's scotch broom.

· The Six Rivers of Gold ·

The six major rivers of the Mother Lode, once so richly laden with gold, offer much more today than hopeful panning. River recreation couldn't be more abundant. During a good part of the year the rivers invite great streamside camping, fishing, white-water rafting, kayaking, and canoeing, and always they offer the beauty of moving waters.

The first river you encounter traveling from the southern region to the north is the Tuolumne River—a favorite river for rafters, fishermen, and nature lovers. It may have been named from the Indian word *Talmalamne*, which means cluster of stone wigwams. The Indians in that area lived in natural recesses in the rocks.

Originating from the Sierra glaciers some thirteen thousand feet high at Mt. Lyell, the Tuolumne River is a main contributor to the water supplies of San Francisco and parts of its peninsula. In the Sierra the Tuolumne flows through some of California's most beautiful scenery—that in Yosemite National Park and the Stanislaus National Forest. The river continues to just west of Modesto, where it joins the San Joaquin River. Both the Tuolumne River and the Stanislaus were bonanzas for the miners.

The Stanislaus is one of the most visually rewarding rivers in California. More than a hundred miles long, the mighty Stan flows from the ten-thousand-foot level in the Sierra through rugged granite mountains and down to the rich agricultural valley of the San Joaquin River. It passes through Tuolumne, Calaveras, and Stanislaus counties.

The river was named after an Indian whose Christian name was Stanislas, after the Polish saint, and who after deserting Mission San Jose was credited with responsibility for an Indian rebellion in the San Joaquin Valley. Gen. Mariano Vallejo arrested him in a bloody battle at the river, which was later named after the brave Indian warrior. John C. Frémont Americanized the spelling to "Stanislaus."

The Stanislaus is one of the most picturesque and exciting white-water rivers, rated with the Colorado and Salmon Rivers for rafting expeditions. Recently, however, the Melones Dam has backed up several miles of the white water, which limits the rafting. But the dam is forming the New Melones Lake, a popular recreation area in its own right.

One stretch recommended for picnics, fishing, and just being at peace in nature's beauty is the Clark Fork branch of the Stanislaus, which is off Highway 108 just north of Strawberry. Late in spring the water

· **Summer magic on the Clark Fork branch of the Stanislaus** ·

cascading through the giant granite gorge is a spectacular sight.

Another of the big six "rivers of gold" is the Mokelumne, 130 miles in length. The headwaters of this picturesque river are high in the Sierra, in Alpine County. Far below, the Mokelumne drains into the San Joaquin River. The name comes from *Mukkel,* which was the name of a Miwok Indian tribe's main village, and *umne,* which means people of.

More than ten thousand feet high in the Sierra the North Fork, the Mokelumne's largest branch, flows through luxuriant green meadows dotted by stunning azure lakes, many of them tucked deeply into canyons. Where the Middle, North, and South Forks flow to lower elevations the country is thick with evergreen trees. Several reservoirs on this river developed power as early as the gold rush days. More than $300

million worth of gold was mined from the Amador County area along the Mokelumne River.

Not much remains of the mining camps along the beautiful but short Consumnes River. This name too is derived from Miwok words: *kosum* for salmon, and again, *umne* for people of.

James Marshall's discovery of gold on January 24, 1848, took place on the South Fork of the American River. The three forks of the American, the river where the gold rush began, each flow high in the western slopes of the Sierra, one extending more than a hundred miles. The basin into which it drains measures nearly two thousand miles, northeast of Sacramento.

The American is an excellent river for dredging and gold panning, and is also a favorite with white-water rafters. Especially in summer the opportunities for camping, fishing, and just lolling about

· The Stanislaus River ·

make the wide banks of this scenic river popular.

The last of the six great Mother Lode rivers is the Yuba. General Vallejo claimed the name is derived from the Spanish word *uvas*—grapes—for the wild variety that grew along the riverbanks. John Sutter said that he named the river in 1840 for an Indian tribe. Whatever the

truth about its name, the facts about its riches are that since 1848 the Yuba and its tributaries have been the source of more gold than any other river system in the United States, and that where the Yuba flows through Downieville and Sierra City, at the northern end of Highway 49, it passes some of the prettiest country in the Mother Lode.

· Coloma's Post Office ·

Situated next to the El Dorado National Forest, the Georgetown area is well timbered and green. Rose gardens front well-kept Victorians; there are many attractive buildings in this quiet town.

The 1859 Balzar House was a three-story dance hall, then an opera house, and in 1890 became the Odd Fellows Hall. The 1864 Shannon Knox House is notable for being built entirely from wood shipped around the Horn from the East. And the old Georgetown Hotel, which is a Victorian inn, is also a well-known dining spot. These buildings have evaded the nemesis of destruction by fire; Georgetown's Main Street was made a hundred feet wide as one precautionary measure.

Backtrack to Highway 49, then drive four miles north to the city of Auburn. In May 1848 a friend of James Marshall named Claude Chana who was on his way to Coloma stopped along the American River in the Auburn Ravine to try his luck at panning. To his surprise he came up with three nuggets right away. The area was one of the richest in the Mother Lode.

Since its tent-city beginnings Auburn has grown to be one of the largest cities along Highway 49, as well as the seat of Placer County. Auburn's setting, in the mountains that surround the American River gorge, is especially beautiful.

When Interstate 80 was put through town it brought a real growth boom to the city, but its construction destroyed many of Auburn's historic buildings. In recent years the town has done a remarkable job of restoring the "Old Town" section; Auburn has undergone a historic revival and is now a national historic landmark. Stop by the local chamber of commerce office on Commercial Street for an excellent walking-tour map of Old Town Auburn.

Auburn's most outstanding example of architecture is the stately domed courthouse, established in 1849. As you walk through Old Town you'll see the four-story, red and white 1893 Hook and Ladder Company Firehouse. Auburn's Volunteer Fire Department was founded in 1852 and claims to be the oldest this side of

Boston. The Placer County Historical Museum, in the fairgrounds on High Street, has fine replicas of gold-rush–era rooms.

Auburn has many historic buildings and boutiques and a number of notable eating establishments. For a memorable dinner try Butterworth's Dining, in an old Victorian at Lincoln Way and Court Street. The English prime rib with Yorkshire pudding is a popular dish served here in an elegant English-American setting. The Old Auburn Hotel serves hearty family-style Basque fare at a set price. For a quick, casual snack try Chef Rizal's House of Chicken and Ribs on Washington Street. If you're not in the mood for the barbeque you can always fill up on the delicious wonton and eggrolls. ■

· Emmanual Episcopal Church in Coloma, dating from 1856 ·

· Malakoff Diggins State Historic Park ·

5

Gold Hill and Humbug Creek

· Mother Lode mare ·

**GRASS VALLEY
TO
MALAKOFF DIGGINS
STATE PARK**

*G*RASS VALLEY IS TWENTY-FOUR MILES NORTH OF AUBURN ALONG HIGHWAY 49. It was 1849 when a company of miners from Boston panned Wolf Creek here, and soon the area became the richest gold mining region in California. In 1850 gold-bearing quartz was discovered on a hill; "Gold Hill" was mined just below the surface to the tune of more than $2 million. Some time later unsophisticated equipment and lack of technology rendered Grass Valley a worked-out camp. Part of the problem was the costly setup efficient quartz mining required. Soon, mines throughout the area were consolidated under three major operations: the Idaho-Maryland, the North Star, and the Empire Mine. The combined revenues were the answer to the expense of quartz mining, which then developed into a major industry, eventually producing $415 million. The great Empire Mine operated for more than a hundred years, in 1931 employing eight hundred people in two shifts. The total number of gold taken out of the giant maze—367 miles of underground tunnels—was 8.5 million ounces. The eighty-stamp mill ran twenty-four hours a day with each 1,750-pound stamp slamming down 104 times a minute. It made such an incredible racket that residents claim people as far away as Nevada City could foretell a shift in the weather by the change of the wind, and the changing sound of the stamps. Obviously this was one of the reasons the family of the owner, William Bourn, didn't live on the grounds full time.

The Empire Mine is now part of the state park system, and the tour offered here is one of the most rewarding you can take. An excellent guide not only takes you to the settings of a typical day in the life of a late-1800s Cornish miner, but helps you vividly relive it. Many of the miners here came from Cornwall, England, where they had worked the tin mines. According to rumor every

Cornishman needed a helper and inevitably recommended as the perfect man for the job "my cousin Jack." Hence the Cornish miners were called cousin jacks.

A real high point of the park tour is the gorgeous Bourn Cottage and surrounding grounds, where William Bourn stayed and entertained when he was visiting the massive operation. It was designed by San Francisco architect Willis Polk, who also designed Bourn's Filoli Estates in Woodside, California. (Mr. Bourn's

motto was "*fight, love and live*": *Filoli*.) Only on the tour can you see the perfect clear-heart redwood rooms, all hand dressed and beautifully appointed with the original furnishings. Surrounded by formal English rose gardens (all the roses pre-1929 varieties), ponds, and fountains, this so-called cottage is an elegant mansion, Grass Valley's pride.

Just out lower Mill Street, in Boston Ravine, you'll find an extensive and impressive array of mining methods on display. Originally the North Star

· **The Bourn Cottage at the Empire Mine in Grass Valley** ·

· **Antique gas pump at Empire Mine** ·

Mine Power Station, today the building is the Nevada County Historical Mining Museum. Among its features are a thirty-foot 1896 Pelton Wheel, the largest of its kind, and many superb exhibits of gold rush artifacts.

Not far away, down Allison Ranch Road, is the eerie foundation ruin of a sixty-stamp mill once part of North Star Mine No. 2. It oddly resembles a giant piece of Aztec or Egyptian architecture.

In spite of the many fires that have plagued Grass Valley, the town's still

· Screen door at Empire Mine ·

· Ruins of North Star Mine sixty-stamp mill in Grass Valley ·

known for its lovely Victorians, and in its residential and business districts the old successfully mixes with the new. A visit to the chamber of commerce will guide you to many historical homes of special note, but the first place that comes to most people's minds when you mention houses is the famous Lola Montez residence. Located at the corner of Mill and Walsh streets, it's well marked and easy to find.

Another pretty and historic side trip is the Highway 29 route out of Grass Valley to the communities of Rough and Ready, Smartville, and Timbucktoo. Who could pass up towns with names as vivid as these? The countryside is rural and quiet, and the towns are small yet quaintly western, and the ghostly spirit of the gold rush still lingers here.

Even though Rough and Ready is just a sleepy little town today, with a couple of stores and a few very old landmarks, it was quite a wild and colorful place once and certainly earned its name. Founded by Mexican War veterans, and named after General Zachary "Rough and Ready" Taylor, this town actually seceded from the Union during the Civil War in protest of a miners' tax.

Smartville was named for James Smart, who ran a hotel there in 1856. Although not much is left to see, it was an active town in the days of hydraulic mining.

The once-successful stage stop Timbucktoo is said to be named after an African who was one of its first miners. Today all that's left is the ruins of a Wells Fargo building.

· **Firehouse No. 1 cupola in Nevada City** ·

Trek back to Highway 49 to go on to Nevada City, four miles north of Grass Valley. Nevada City is probably the most attractive of the larger Mother Lode towns. Like Rome and San Francisco, the town was built on seven hills. Their names over the years have been variously Aristocracy, Piety, Lost, Boulder, Bourbon, American, and Nabob, and at one time some were called Oregon, Buckeye, Wet, and Cement Hills. When miners first started placer mining here in 1849 on Deer Creek the settlement was called Deer Creek Dry Diggins. Then it named itself Nevada. After the territory of Nevada was established in 1861, and increasingly when the State of Nevada took the name, there was much protest. The outcome was the addition of the word city to the town name, alleviating postal confusion.

By 1850, six thousand prospectors were in the vicinity. Even so, Nevada City was a more organized and law-abiding town than most, owing to the strong influence of its New Englander populace. No town in the Mother Lode in the 1850s suffered greater or more frequent devastation from fires and flood than Nevada City. Yet thanks to the abundance of gold, pride, and incredible stamina, the townspeople never gave up. Each catastrophe was followed by rebuilding with more brick structures.

Today's Nevada City retains much of the old town's flavor, with winding streets and many stately Victorian homes embellished by picket fences, gazebos, and peaceful gardens. The main thoroughfare in town is gas-lamp-lined Broad Street, fronting the famous National Hotel. This is a different famous National Hotel from the ones in Jamestown and Jackson but, like them, it is highly recommended. Also offering gold-rush-era atmosphere, in a lovely garden setting, is the gingerbreaded Red Castle Inn.

Just off Broad Street on Main Street is the photogenic 1861 Firehouse No. 1, now the handsome home of the Nevada City Museum. The museum has a collection of early gold rush attire and even some artifacts from the Donner Party, as well as the ornate, period trimmings of the building itself. To locate several other historic buildings pick up a walking-tour map from the chamber of commerce, on Main Street. A walk through the Pioneer Cemetery conveys history on a personal level.

Nevada City has a wonderful gourmet Mexican restaurant, with the accent

· Sierra thistle ·

more on gourmet than on Mexican. What Framastanyl's offers is not authentic old Mexican, but the deviations are all delicious and satisfying. Try lunch on the pleasant patio or a romantic dinner in the intimate dining room.

From Nevada City to Downieville several routes present themselves. If you stick with 49 you can turn off for a run deeper into the country, see a covered bridge, and then continue on the highway. Alternatively you can take a winding and adventurous route

· Downtown Nevada City ·

· Lola Montez and Lotta Crabtree ·

Lola Montez, born Eliza Gilbert in Ireland in 1818, came to the Gold Country to dazzle the miners with her shocking tarantula dance and her beauty. She had been a European theater sensation and mistress to several famous men. Among them were Alexandre Dumas, Victor Hugo, Franz Liszt, and "Mad" King Ludwig of Bavaria, whom she left when Bavaria was undergoing a revolution.

Unfortunately Montez was just a passable actress and at best a mediocre dancer. After disappointing first the San Franciscans and then residents of Sacramento and Marysville, she decided to give up her theater career, and she moved to Grass Valley with her pet monkeys and bears. (Supposedly she evicted one husband—Pat Hull—for shooting one of the bears.)

In her house on Mill Street in Grass Valley Lola Montez helped train her young friend Lotta Crabtree as a song-and-dance girl. And generally she led a social, carefree life for about two years. But then problems intruded. She clashed with the editor of the *Grass Valley Telegraph,* Henry Shipley; he had published a story noting that Lola was not particularly popular among the ladies and many of the gentlemen in town. She publicly and personally horse-whipped him. Shipley left town humiliated, and later he committed suicide.

Soon after this incident Montez became bored and, missing the elegance of her previous lifestyle, decided to try Australia for a change. It was from Australia in 1855 that the report filtered back of Lola's plans to become empress of California. It was rumored she was plotting for California to secede from the Union, whereupon she would establish an empire and have herself crowned. All she accomplished on her return to California was marrying two more husbands. Eventually Lola Montez lost her health and wealth, and she spent her last days in rescue work among women in New York City. She died in 1861 at the age of forty-three.

Lotta Crabtree may have learned more than performance techniques from the example of her teacher, Lola Montez. After quickly picking up a few songs and dances, Lotta traveled the gold camp circuit with her business-manager mother plus a drummer and a fiddler. Dressed in green knickers, green coat, and matching high hat, she sang Irish ballads and danced gaily, delighting the nineteenth-century miners. Her debut, in Rough and Ready, was at age eight.

Crabtree was smart enough not to go traipsing off to Australia with Montez, and she grew ever more popular with the miners. They showed their appreciation by literally showering her with gold. The wholesome joy she conveyed made her the most beloved of all the traveling entertainers in the gold rush days, and she also became a successful stage actress in San Francisco. Lotta Crabtree lived a rich, full life, and left an estate totalling $4 million.

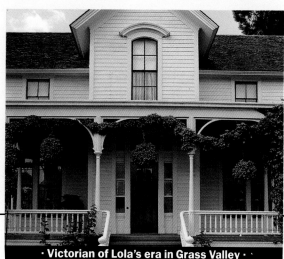

· **Victorian of Lola's era in Grass Valley** · ·

north that also leads by Malakoff Diggins State Park. Or, by backtracking a few miles between jogs off Highway 49, you can combine the two, as described here.

The first leg of the combination route is a fourteen-mile run up Highway 49 to the Pleasant Valley Road turnoff and thence to French Corral and Bridgeport. Though there's not much to see in French Corral, a tiny town named for the mule corral built there by a Frenchman in 1849, what there is stands proud. The single old structure is the iron-doored brick Wells Fargo building and community center, so close to the road no one could miss it. French Corral's biggest contribution to history is in being the site of the state's first cross-country phone. It was installed by the Milton Mining and Water Company and joined the company headquarters there with French Lake, nearly sixty miles away. In French Corral wild sweet peas grow profusely along the roadsides.

Two miles farther on is Bridgeport and the longest single-span covered bridge in the United States. Stretching across the South Fork of the Yuba River, it has quite a visual impact. The bridge was built by David I. Wood in 1862 and for thirty-nine years was used by freight trains carrying supplies to the Northern Mines and Comstock Lode in Nevada to cross the river on a turnpike toll route. It was actually open for public use from 1901 to 1971, when it was judged unsafe. The new bridge that now crosses the river nearby offers a fine vantage point for viewing this monumental covered bridge.

Next, return to Highway 49, backtrack south two miles, and take the Tyler–Foote Crossing Road into Malakoff Diggins State Park. Though Tyler–Foote Crossing Road is only partly paved it is easily accessible. Besides, the deep ravines along the way are full of evergreens and ferns, and in spring dogwood trees are in blossom there. Every mile of the sixteen is worth the drive. (The rugged piece of road is beyond the park.)

After you pass through North Columbia and Lake City you come to North Bloomfield, located at the park's center. First called Humbug in 1851 by unlucky miners, the town was renamed North Bloomfield in 1857. By 1880, 1,229 people were living here. It once had seven saloons and two breweries, perhaps accounting for the Clampers' apparent fondness for this town.

North Bloomfield has been restored to its guise of the gold rush days and has several buildings you can look into and see the old-fashioned business establishments. Unlike those at Columbia State Park, the businesses here are no longer active. For the attention to historic detail tour such buildings as the drugstore, King Saloon, McKilligan and Mobley General Merchandise Store, post office, blacksmith shop, and fire station. There's also an E Clampus Vitus building. The Clampers had quite an impact here; they even have a spot called the Clampicnic area.

Peaceful meadows and trails surround North Bloomfield. Take a walk to Humbug Creek or the trail to the old 1872 schoolhouse, with the old books and wooden desks intact. An excellent

· Giant monitor nozzle in North Bloomfield ·

· Stamp mill in Grass Valley ·

· Drug store and saloon in North Bloomfield ·

· **Hydraulicked landscape near Malakoff Diggins** ·

museum explains hydraulic mining so you can fully comprehend what you see when you enter the diggins.

Malakoff Diggins has excellent examples of the giant monitor nozzles once used for hydraulic mining. The miners who blasted away the earth from the mountainsides with high-pressure streams of water through these monitors literally changed the forms of the land and, with it, the environmental balance of nature. To convey the water to the site, the North Bloomfield Mining and Gravel Company used an elaborate system of flumes and canals. The drainage tunnel dug was seventy-eight hundred feet long. The amount of energy expended to set up such a drastic method—and the determination of the miners who employed it—nearly defies comprehension. But then hard-rock mining, which is digging networks of underground tunnels, is just as strenuous—just not quite as damaging to the environment.

Hydraulic mining caused erosion, polluted streams, killed fish, and flooded the rich agricultural valleys. This continued until 1884, when the method was outlawed. Ironically, what remains at Malakoff Diggins is more than an impressive commentary on man's sometimes reckless impact on the environment, although certainly it is that. It also is beautiful. In fact it's a sixteen-hundred-acre wonder.

The mountainsides here are like a miniature Grand Canyon, with variegated shades of rust tipping statuesque white formations. The rocks are particularly attractive and surreal-

· The Old Graveyards and Churches ·

Perhaps the most conspicuous testimony to the pioneers is in the charming old churches that were early erected in the Mother Lode and in the region's many graveyards. When you wander among lichen-covered headstones, the awareness of history is noticeably heightened. Some of the graves, weedy and overgrown, are still enclosed by ornate if weathered wrought-iron fences.

Most of the markers in the old plots date from the late 1800s and early 1900s. In some instances members of entire families, including young children, were buried within months of each other, apparently victims of the same disease. And there are headstones for many mothers who died in childbirth and the infants who joined them a month or so later.

One impressive gravestone in the Pioneer Cemetary at Nevada City marks the grave of Henry Meredith, born in Hanover County, Virginia, on August 14, 1826. He died in battle across the Sierra at Pyramid Lake, in what was then Utah Territory, on May 12, 1860. His epitaph is composed of his last words, when he was wounded and offered assistance to safety: "No! Leave me here. I might put you in peril."

A particularly unusual grave marker is in the cemetary at Hornitos, just behind the old church on the hill. The stone is formed in the shape of the trunk of an oak, with acorns and leaves ornately decorating the sides. At the top the epitaph reads simply: "Edward S. Adams— Here rests a woodsman of the world."

Such preaching as was irregularly heard in the early mining camps was done by circuit-riding parsons, who erected makeshift pulpits to spread the word of salvation. Eventually, as the camps settled into more stable townships, churches were erected, and the traveling preacher became part of the past.

The architectural designs of the permanent places of worship were influenced primarily by the settlers from New England. In many of the small gold towns the churches are the most historic and starkly beautiful of the remaining buildings. As a result, the churches and old graveyards of the Mother Lode are popular photographic subjects.

· St. Francis Xavier Catholic Church in Chinese Camp ·

istic at sunset and sunrise. On the valley floor you walk over unearthly piles of rocks, and interspersed in the manzanita and wildflowers are such signs of the past as rusted old pieces broken off the great iron flumes, piled together like forgotten rubbish yet of a piece with the landscape. Now the site has a reed-filled deep marsh pond, studded with colorful odd rocks, and it's home to many wild birds.

To take your time getting to know this special park, camp in one of the scenic campgrounds above the diggins. Campsites are surrounded by towering ponderosa pines and have large wood-burning fire pits, picnic tables, storage cabinets, and nearby restrooms.

To continue the backroads route north proceed on Tyler–Foote Crossing Road out of North Columbia. This route passes through Alleghany (where you can see the Kenton Mine Lodge) and the town of Forest on the way to Downieville. On the map, Tyler–Foote Crossing Road looks to be the shorter route than returning to Highway 49 before veering north. It might be shorter, but it takes considerably longer.

If you like rugged country roads, you'll love this route to Alleghany. At stretches this road gets narrow and rough and in spots downright treacherous. On one side you look straight down what appears to be a bottomless canyon, and on the other you look at a rock-walled bank and wonder whether your car isn't passing it too closely. Try this road in a compact car or four-wheel-drive vehicle. Definitely don't try it with a trailer.

On the positive side, a wealth of wildflowers grows along Tyler–Foote Crossing Road's banks, making the slow going a real pleasure. Among them are Indian pink, monkeyflowers, tidytips, paintbrush, larkspur, stonecrop (a succulent), Western wallflowers, Sierra iris, common groundsel, and purple thistles. Looking off the canyon side is dizzying but breathtaking; far downhill is the rushing Yuba River, and thickly wooded valleys and mountains alternate as far as you can see.

Alleghany is like none of the gold towns in the rest of the Mother Lode. Its houses, which are mostly wooden, are built on the hillside around windy streets. The town was supported mainly by the famous mine called Sixteen to One, named after one of the presidential campaign slogans for William Jennings Bryan. Although not much of the mine is left to be seen, it had a very high grade ore and yielded $26 million in gold before it was closed in 1965.

If you've made it this far you must visit the Kenton Mine Lodge, down the road just a bit farther. It's run by Al Weiss. Situated at the bottom of a canyon next to Kanaka Creek, the lodge consists of restored cottages and a bunkhouse that was actually the miners' housing at the old Kenton Mine, operated from 1860 to 1939. The furnishings are down-home-style antiques, some of which were made by the miners themselves.

Aside from exploring one of the oldest hard-rock mines in the Northern Mines area, you can spend your time at the Kenton Mine Lodge panning at the creek, hiking, fishing, or getting to know other guests over the big home-cooked family-style meals. Staying here is a very casual and relaxing way to unwind and enjoy yourself.

On the way to Forest in the spring you see many dogwoods in blossom. Forest is a quiet little town, and as though to emphasize this quality almost all the old buildings and houses on the main road through town have been painted the same pinkish brown color. The residents number fewer than thirty. You can tell they're not used to lots of visitors by the way they watch the passers-through, but they're friendly.

A couple of mineshaft openings along the Oregon Creek in town are picturesque. The Sixteen to One Mine Company owns these mines, but they're not being worked at present. One of the shaft entrances is a real jewel when seen close up; the water in the tunnel provides perfect conditions for the growth of a lush moss carpet and water plants on the rock walls near the head frame. And as with other tunnels, the opening offers natural underground refrigeration. Not a bad place to take a break on a hot summer day.

Next wind your way north to the junction with Highway 49. A few miles east is Downieville. ■■■■■

· **Blacksmith shop in North Bloomfield** ·

6

Majestic Mountains and Glacier Lakes

· High Sierra sunset in the pines ·

**DOWNIEVILLE
TO
PLUMAS-EUREKA
STATE PARK**

*T*HE NORTHERNMOST PART OF THE MOTHER LODE, IN STARK CONTRAST TO THE typical oak-covered foothills elsewhere, is in the high Sierra. Nestled in majestic, pine-covered mountains, Downieville sits at one of the highest elevations in the state. The town itself is particularly attractive in the true, uncontrived old-West tradition. In 1849 a Scot named William Downie discovered gold where two forks of the Yuba River came together and shortly afterward built a cabin there with some other prospectors. This was the beginning of a prosperous gold camp. Miners referred to it as "Tincup Diggins," because a day's work usually produced a cupful. And, for obvious reasons, at one time the town also was called The Forks. In the winter of 1849 many miners, not used to the heavy snows in the Northern Mines, died of starvation or cold. Their small canvas tents collapsed under each big snowstorm. But new miners continually arrived, and for those who stuck it out the effort paid off handsomely. In one year nearly a quarter million dollars in gold was taken from just a mile of diggins at Good Year's Bar. According to historical accounts, Downieville had such rich diggins that even in this rugged, remote high country the miners and residents could afford to be choosy about what they ate and drank. One Judge Edward W. McIlhany paid three thousand dollars to have packed in for his pleasure sea-bird

· **Lunch break in Downieville at the Hirschfeldter Building** ·

eggs stored in lime, plus wines, liquors, cigars, and tobacco, in addition to canned goods.

At one time Downieville had more than five thousand residents, many substantial homes, a theater, several saloons, a gambling house, and fandango dance halls. If you dig deeper into the town's history you'll find stories of duels, gunfights, and "sudden deaths." Along the crooked streets of today's Downieville, you will find many historic buildings; the ones that have survived are built of stone.

· **Windows at the Kentucky Mine** ·

· The Kentucky Mine north of Sierra City ·

· Sierra City architecture ·

· Private home in Downieville ·

California's oldest continuously operating newspaper, the *Mountain Messenger,* has been read by the residents of Sierra, Nevada, and Plumas Counties since 1853, and the building that houses the paper itself dates from 1852.

Two stores in town also occupy historic structures: the Craycroft and Hirschfeldter Buildings, both built in 1852. The myriad artifacts displayed at the wonderful museum, also built in 1852, include oxen yokes, nineteenth-century clothing, and a full-size, cutaway yellowjacket nest. A

one-to-six scale model shows the workings of a stamp mill, and several old oil paintings depict local high-Sierra scenes. It's fun to browse here. When you've completed a walking tour try The Forks, right on the main street, for a hearty lunch or dinner. Downieville is a relaxed locale; it's visited for the gold panning, fishing, camping, hiking, and for the crisp mountain air.

Author and local historian James B. Sinnott was born and raised in Downieville. He has published a set of seven

books that bring together old photographs, personal letters, diaries, bills of sale, newspaper clippings, and stories accurately depicting the gold rush days of Sierra County. Published by Mid-Cal of Fresno, the volumes are so popular they are considered collector's items. In conversation Sinnott related his most vivid memory: Armistice Day, November 11, 1918. At the end of World War I everyone in Downieville was intensely patriotic. A huge street bonfire crackled in the midst of wild carrying on, and a man they all called Frenchie perched atop

· Flourishing Business ·

Many types of businesses flourished during the gold rush. The prices of goods fluctuated according to supply and demand just as they do today but reacted to extremes with ridiculous effect. When something basic, such as potatoes, became scarce, suddenly the problem would completely reverse itself; so many people would grow potatoes locally that when cargoes from the East finally arrived in San Francisco they were worthless, and were dumped in the Bay or left to rot. Conversely, a commodity that filled one of the many critical needs that arose, partic-ularly in high, remote gold camps, was almost beyond price. For one jar of the raisins used to treat scurvy, miners were known to pay as much as four thousand dollars. Early in the rush so much gold was exchanged that its value relative to that of the staples of life became almost negligible. The following itemized breakfast tab was paid by E. Gould Buffam in Coloma in the summer of 1848:

Sardines (1 tin)	*$16.00*
1 lb. hard bread	*2.00*
1 lb. butter	*6.00*
½ lb. cheese	*3.00*
2 bottles of ale	*16.00*
	$43.00

Only six months later most staples were sold for not much more than $1.00 a pound.

Other commodities that were money-makers were the common tools of the prospectors, including picks, shovels, pans, wheelbarrows, and sturdy clothing—which consisted mainly of wide-brimmed hats, flannel shirts, leather boots, and denim trousers.

Levi Strauss grabbed his opportunity for success when he designed pants specifically to meet the miners' needs. Levi came from New York to San Francisco by ship in 1850, bringing with him cloth from his brother's shop. He had heard miners were having troubles with their trousers, tearing them easily in the rugged working conditions of the camps. Using tent canvas, Levi made a pair of pants for a miner that became a popular notion overnight—word quickly spread about "the pants of Levi." His brother shipped more heavy denim material, and Levi dyed it blue.

An old miner named Alkali Ike complained about his pockets ripping at the corners when he stuffed them with heavy ore pieces. A Nevada tailor eliminated that problem by having a harness maker reinforce the pocket corners with copper rivets. When Levi heard of this, he hired the tailor and patented the rivet solution. And he continued to prove his talent for recognizing good ideas. His practical denims eventually caught on throughout the entire Southwest, and Levi became known as the cowboy's tailor.

In the new communities, skilled workmen, mechanics, and professionals prospered. Because of the need for living structures, brick-layers and carpenters, too, did very well, but for all there was an easy downfall. To succeed in business, one had to resist the lure of prospecting.

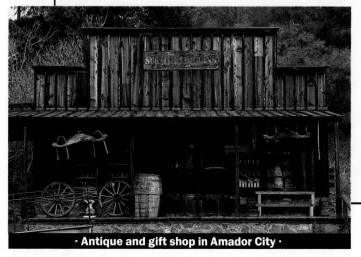

· **Antique and gift shop in Amador City** ·

· The Yuba River ·

the bell tower and sang "La Marseillaise" at the top of his voice. That was a joyful celebration. This historian also told of his uncle's attempt in 1850 to sway the majority opinion at the infamous Juanita's murder trial, falsely testifying that she was with child. Juanita was hung anyway—a black mark Downieville carried for many years afterward.

A thirteen-mile scenic drive east leads to Sierra City, at the northern end of the Mother Lode. Highway 49 along the Yuba River runs through deep canyons, frequently passing lush vegtation and small waterfalls. As you enter Sierra City your attention is instantly drawn to the ragged Sierra Buttes that tower above. This town's setting is the most spectacular of any in the high Sierra.

Founded in 1850, Sierra City was built on the rich finds of the Sierra Buttes Mine. This area was full of productive diggins with a high grade of gold. History tells of a gold nugget found here in 1869 weighing an incredible 141 pounds. An impressive collection of handsome nuggets from Sierra City is on permanent display at the museum in San Francisco's United States Mint. Unlike the other mining towns (with their disastrous fires), Sierra City's devastating hazard was the snow avalanches that literally crushed the town, taking many lives. The worst of these catastrophes occurred in 1852, 1888, and again in 1889.

Sierra City's oldest building dates back to 1860. The Zerloff Hotel, housing the only saloon left of the many that operated during the gold rush, stands at the end of main street as you enter town. A more modern place to stay or dine that features an inspiring view

· Live tamarack pine in the Sierra Buttes ·

of the buttes is the friendly Herrington's Sierra Pines Lodge. For a satisfying breakfast or lunch, stop at the Mountain Shadows.

The Sierra Buttes vicinity has many crystal blue glacier lakes; among the most striking are Sardine and Gold Lakes, as well as Sand Pond, each reflecting the surrounding mountains. The rugged unexploited beauty here commands respect.

Snowmobiles offer access to the quiet snowy wilderness of the high buttes. The owners of the Mountain Shad-

· Store front in Johnsville ·

· Reflections of the Sierra Buttes in Sand Pond Lake ·

ows, Tom and Demaris Harbart, sell and rent the equipment necessary for deep-woods exploration.

Before you leave Sierra City tour the monumental Kentucky Mine, only a quarter mile north of town. Built in the later 1850s, the five-stamp mill here, which operated off and on until 1944, is in excellent restored condition, the giant wooden housing and equipment still intact. The museum on the grounds has outstanding displays of local artifacts.

For one last side trip, turn off Highway 49 just beyond the Kentucky Mine; take Gold Lake Road north seven miles toward Johnsville and the Plumas-Eureka State Park. The well-maintained highway runs through rugged rocky, wooded mountains. Be sure to take the short turnoffs along the way to view the lakes on the west side of the road; the storybook settings for these sparkling glacier lakes are a photographer's dream, and for camping and fishing enthusiasts they're a paradise.

Following Gold Lake Road to the city of Graeagle, you come to a turnoff for

Road A14 toward Plumas-Eureka State Park. Among the old mining equipment found throughout the park is a fine example of a forty-eight-stamp mill in a multistoried old wooden building. The park museum has drawings and graphs showing the numerous shafts dug in the area, as well as memorabilia from the 1870s.

Johnsville, which was built in the 1870s by a London-based investment company and is now in the state park, offers the sight of an unusual juxtaposition. Dilapidated wooden structures look like remnants of a ghost town, left to decay, but right alongside are elegant restored residences and brand-new luxurious homes. One restaurant in town, the Iron Door, is romantically decorated and offers a superb dining menu. The unrestored old structures have a lot of loose debris that makes wandering inside unsafe, but they're quite photogenic and it's fun to snoop around them. Johnsville is a picturesque community, and the drive to it and the park are worth the extra miles at the end of your trip through the Mother Lode.

· Melting ice cover at Gold Lake in early spring ·

· Juanita ·

She is remembered as a lady of ill repute, but the people who condemned her to death got more bad press over the years than she did. Known as Juanita, she was the only woman ever to be hung in the Mother Lode. Today, punishment for what Juanita did would probably be mitigated; it was a crime of passion. But nevertheless it was a crime.

Juanita was a proud lady of Spanish-Mexican descent and a pretty dance-hall girl. In 1850, during a drunken July Fourth celebration in Downieville, a man named Jack Cannon stumbled inebriated and uninvited through the door of the tiny adobe residence occupied by Juanita and her lover. A companion of the drunken intruder removed him without further incident. The next morning Cannon supposedly went back to apologize, but Juanita's Latin temper had been steaming all night, and she answered his apology with a dagger thrust into his throat.

News of the tragic murder quickly spread through town, and an angry mob came for Juanita. She went before them adorned in her best jewels and prettiest dress, in preparation. The impromptu lynch mob held a sort of court and acquitted the lover. Juanita, however, although she pleaded self-defense, was sentenced to hang from a makeshift scaffold by the river.

Her quiet and dignified words, as she put the noose around her neck and jumped from the platform to her death, were simply, "Adios, Señores."

· Downieville's wild rose ·

· The Sierra Buttes ·

· Mother Lode Chambers of Commerce ·

These area chambers of commerce can help you obtain more complete information about what each county in the Mother Lode has to offer.

Mariposa County Chamber of Commerce
P.O. Box 425
Mariposa, CA 95338
(209) 966-2456

Tuolumne County Chamber of Commerce
P.O. Box 277
Sonora, CA 95370
(209) 532-4212

Calaveras County Chamber of Commerce
P.O. Box 177
San Andreas, CA 95249
(209) 754-3391

Amador County Chamber of Commerce

P.O. Box 596
Jackson, CA 95642
(209) 223-0350

El Dorado County Chamber of Commerce
542 Main Street
Placerville, CA 95667
(916) 626-2344

Placer County Chamber of Commerce
661 Newcastle Road

Newcastle, CA 95658
(916) 663-2061

Nevada City Chamber of Commerce
132 Main Street
Nevada City, CA 95959
(916) 265-2692

Sierra County Chamber of Commerce
P.O. Box 555
Downieville, CA 95936
(No phone)

· El Dorado County Chamber of Commerce in Placerville ·

· Recommended Inns ·

These inns, listed south to north, have rates ranging from quite inexpensive to moderately expensive. Rooms should be reserved in advance.

Jamestown

National Hotel
In operation since 1859, this historic hotel was refurbished in 1981. The light, airy rooms are nicely furnished with antiques. A continental breakfast is served; on weekends a hot breakfast is available in the dining room or on the outdoor patio shaded by 100-year-old grapevines. This restaurant specializes in Italian/American cuisine and offers lunch and dinner daily. On Main Street. (209) 984-3446.

Jamestown Hotel
This elegant hotel was completely remodeled in 1982. The suites and rooms are quite tastefully appointed with antiques, fine wallpapers, and private Victorian baths. The hotel serves a continental breakfast in bed. The restaurant serves lunch, dinner, and Sunday champagne brunch. It also has a beautiful saloon, heavy on the oak and brass. On Main Street. (209) 984-3902.

Sonora

The Gunn House
Many of the antique-furnished rooms here are near the private swimming pool or the elegant lounge. This inn, built around 1850, has a lot of ambiance, and the atmosphere is restful in spite of the location right on the main street. Continental breakfast is included with the room. At 286 Washington Street. (209) 532-3421.

The Sonora Inn
Recently refurbished, this hotel has spacious rooms, a swimming pool and sauna, a steak and seafood restaurant, and a separate coffee shop. The cocktail lounge frequently has live music. Located on the corner of Highway 108 and Washington Street, near the entrance to town. (209) 532-7468.

Columbia

The City Hotel
Built in 1856, this fine old hotel has pleasantly antique-furnished rooms, all with half baths. The attractive sitting parlor is a nice place to meet other travelers over your continental breakfast. Just below, on the first level of the hotel, the gourmet dining room serves brunch, lunch, and dinner; the meals are exceptional experiences in themselves. On Main Street. (209) 532-1479.

Murphys

Murphys Hotel and Lodge
Built in 1856, this hotel has a beautiful setting and offers antique-furnished rooms that recently have been restored. There's an elegant dining room open for breakfast, lunch, and dinner featuring a wide variety of dishes. A large picturesque saloon has handsome western furnishings. Right on the main street of Murphys. (209) 728-3444.

Mokelumne Hill

Hotel Leger
Built in 1851, this charming old hotel has rooms furnished with antiques; some rooms have fireplaces and private baths. There's a great frontier-style saloon and good restaurant. Other amenities include a garden setting, swimming pool, and porches for relaxing. Adjacent is the Court House Theater, where you can catch a good play on Saturday nights. Located on the main street as you enter town. (209) 286-1401.

Jackson

National Hotel
This hotel was built in 1862, and has a real old-West atmosphere. The rooms are antique furnished, and a colorful saloon with a 100-year-old bar and restaurant is adjacent. At 2 Water Street. (209) 223-0500.

Volcano

St. George Hotel
Built in 1862, this three-story charmer is nicely decorated, with antiques, a piano, and a fireplace downstairs; the balconies are nice for people watching or just taking it easy. The restaurant is a good one. On the main street as you enter town. (209) 296-4458.

Sutter Creek

Sutter Creek Inn
This inn, dating from about 1865, is the most unusually furnished you'll find, offering some rooms with beds swinging by chains, some with romantic fireplaces or even a piano. The whole is very tastefully done, in a gorgeous garden setting. Breakfast is served in a large country kitchen. Staying here brings out the romantic in guests. At 75 Main Street. (209) 267-5606.

· **The Blair Room in Jackson's Court Street Inn** ·

Operating since 1852, the hotel has beautifully furnished rooms with lots of antiques and a rich Victorian atmosphere. Well known for the excellent weekend brunches, the dining room is open daily for breakfast, lunch, and dinner. The hotel itself is very attractive and has become quite a landmark. At 211 Broad Street. (916) 265-4551.

Red Castle Inn
Built in 1860, the Red Castle's ornate architecture is trimmed in white icicle-type gingerbread and is surrounded by wonderful gardens with lots of places to sit and relax. The furnishings are antique, private baths are available, and continental breakfast is included. At 109 Prospect Street. (916) 265-5135.

Sierra City

Herrington Sierra Pines Lodge
Rather than historical accommodations, this high-country resort offers a warm modern cabin atmosphere. It's right on the Yuba River, across from a spectacular view of the Sierra Buttes. The restaurant serves a good breakfast, lunch, and dinner daily. On Highway 49 as you enter Sierra City. (916) 289-3243.

Amador

The Mine House Inn
This 1872 building has been converted from what was once the headquarters of the Keystone Mine. It's a real gem, offering refreshing rooms with antique furnishings, all private baths, continental breakfast in bed and a new swimming pool. On the main highway as you enter Amador. (209) 267-5900.

Coloma

Vineyard House
Beautiful gardens surround this lovely old hotel. The rooms are antique furnished with lots of Victorian atmosphere. There's a handsome, well-appointed saloon in the old cellar. A popular brunch and a fine dinner are served in the elegant dining room. Just up Cold Springs Road as you enter Coloma. (916) 622-2217.

Nevada City

National Hotel
This inn is reported to be the oldest in continuous operation in California.

· Bibliography ·

Alt, David D., and Hyndman, Donald W. *Roadside Geology of Northern California*. Missoula: Mountain Press, 1975.

Andrews, John R. *The Ghost Towns of Amador*. New York: Carlton Press, 1978.

Andrews, Peter, and Allen, George. *California: A Guide to the Inns of California*. Los Angeles, Knapp Press, 1980.

Atherton, Gertrude. *Golden Gate Country*. New York: Duell, 1945.

Automobile Club of Southern California. *Spanish California and the Gold Rush*. Los Angeles: Automobile Club of Southern California, 1966.

Axon, Gordon V. *The California Gold Rush*. New York: Mason/Charter, 1976.

Ayers, Col. James J. *Gold and Sunshine: Reminiscences of Early California*. Boston: The Gorham Press, 1922.

Chalfant, Willie Arthur. *Gold, Guns & Ghost Towns*. Stanford, Calif.: Stanford University Press, 1947.

Chamberlain, Newell D. *The Call of Gold*. Rev. ed. Santa Cruz: Western Tanager Press, 1972.

Cleland, Robert Glass. *From Wilderness to Empire: A History of California*. New York: Knopf, 1944.

Cook, Fred S. *Legends of the Southern Mines*. Volcano, Calif.: California Traveler, 1971.

Crain, Jim. *Historic Country Inns of California*. San Francisco: Chronicle Books, 1977.

Ferguson, Charles D. *California Gold Fields*. Oakland: Biobooks, 1948.

Glasscock, Carl Burgess. *A Golden Highway*. Indianapolis: Bobbs-Merrill, 1934.

Gudde, Erwin Gustav. *California Gold Camps*. Berkeley: University of California Press, 1975.

Hitchcock, Anthony, and Lindgren, Jean. *Country Inns, Lodges, and Historic Hotels of California & the West*. New York: Burt Franklin and Co., 1982.

Holliday, James S. *The World Rushed In*. New York: Simon and Schuster, 1981.

Hulbert, Archer Butler. *Forty-Niners: The Chronicle of the California Trail*. Boston: Little, Brown & Co., 1931.

Jackson, Donald Dale. *Gold Dust*. New York: Knopf, 1980.

Jackson, Joseph Henry. *Anybody's Gold: The Story of California's Mining Towns*. San Francisco: Chronicle Books, 1970.

Jenkins, Olaf Pitt. *Geologic Guidebook along Highway 49, Sierran Gold Belt. The Mother Lode Country*. California Department of Natural Resources, Division of Mines. Bull. 141. Sacramento: California Department of Natural Resources, 1948.

Johnson, Paul C. *Sierra Album*. Garden City, N.J.: Doubleday, 1971.

Jolly, John. *Gold Spring Diary: The Journal of John Jolly*. Sonora, Calif.: Tuolumne County Historical Society, 1966.

Jones, Paul. *California Gold Country: A Great Escapes Guide for the Mother Lode*. San Francisco: Great Escapes Publications, 1973.

Koenig, George. *Ghosts of the Gold Rush: Being a Wayward Guide to the Mother Lode Country*. Glendale, Calif.: La Siesta Press, 1968.

Lewis, Oscar. *Sea Routes to the Gold Fields: The Migration by Water to California in 1849–1852*. New York: Knopf, 1949.

McGroarty, John S. *California: Its History and Romance*. Los Angeles: Grafton Publishing Co., 1920.

Masri, Allan, and Abenheim, Peter. *The Golden Hills of California: A Descriptive Guide to the Mother Lode Counties of the Southern Mines*. Fresno: Valley Publishers, 1979.

Morgan, Ora. *Gold Dust*. Los Angeles: Frank A. Morgan, 1959.

Morley, Jim. *Gold Cities: Grass Valley & Nevada City*. Berkeley: Howell-North Books, 1965.

Nadeau, Remi. *Ghost Towns and Mining Camps of California*. Los Angeles: Ward Ritchie Press, 1965.

Nadeau, Remi. *The Real Joaquin Murieta: Robin Hood Hero or Gold Rush Gangster?* Corona del Mar, Calif.: Trans-Anglo Books, 1974.

Pacific Gas & Electric Co. *The Rivers of California*. San Francisco: PG&E Publications, 1962.

Paul, Rodman W. *California Gold: The Beginning of Mining in the Far West.* Boston: Harvard University Press, 1947.

Riesenberg, Jr., Felix. *The Golden Road.* New York: McGraw-Hill, 1962.

Schafer, Silvia Anne. *Gold Country.* Whittier, Calif.: Journal Publications, 1977.

Secrest, William B. *Joaquin —Bloody Bandit of the Mother Lode.* Fresno: Saga-West, 1967.

Sinnott, James B. *Sierra City and Goodyears Bar.* Fresno: Mid-Cal Publishers, 1978.

Stellman, Louis J. *The Mother Lode.* San Francisco: Harr Wagner, 1934.

Stone, Irving. *Men to Match My Mountains: The Opening of the Far West.* New York: Doubleday, 1956.

Sunset. *Gold Rush Country.* Menlo Park, Calif.: California Lane Books, 1972.

Time-Life Books. *The Forty-Niners.* New York: Time-Life Books, 1976.

Zauner, Phyllis, and Zauner, Lou. *California Gold.* Tahoe Paradise, Calif.: Zanel Publications, 1980.

· **Courthouse in Mariposa, operating since 1854** ·

· Index ·

· One of the Mother Lode's many magnificent oaks ·

· The Authors ·

Charles Moore began his professional photographic career in 1957 as chief photographer for the Montgomery, Alabama newspapers, winning many awards and recognition for his photojournalism. In 1962, he began his freelance career and became a member of the largest and one of the most prestigious photo agencies in the world, Black Star of New York City, which represents him still today.

In October 1962, Charles shot his first major assignment for *Life* magazine. This led to nearly ten years of contractual assignments for *Life* around the world, covering subjects ranging from revolutions in Latin America to famous Hollywood celebrities. Among the many awards he received for his work were a special citation from the American Society of Magazine Publishers for his civil-rights coverage during the turbulent 60s and an Aviation-Space Writers

Award for his coverage of B-52 raids over Vietnam, where he flew with the U.S. Air Force on combat missions.

Charles relocated to San Francisco from New York City in 1973. Since that time, he has specialized in corporate-industrial and travel photography. Southeast Asia has been his special corner of the world, where he has traveled extensively since 1965.

· The Moores at home in Columbia ·

After moving to Columbia in 1979, and while continuing to travel the world for his corporate-industrial clients, Charles managed to take the time to pursue his personal goals. His natural love and appreciation for nature and land-scapes are expressed in his photographic coverage of the California Mother Lode.

Today, Charles lectures on and teaches photog-raphy, and continues to exhibit his color photography on both the east and west coasts.

■

Born in Oregon, raised in Montana, and transplanted to California in 1963, Kristin Moore's background includes a wide variety of business experiences including several executive positions in the field of graphic design and sales promotion. After over ten years of high-pressure work in the San Francisco Bay Area, she welcomed moving to a small town atmosphere with her husband, Charles, in 1979.

Kristin's deep interest in history and writing were put to the test in this first book, which reflects her love and enthusiasm for her new home, the California Mother Lode. After completion of two years of research and manuscript preparation for this book, she recently formed a design firm in Sonora called *Hart & Moore*.

The Mother Lode was designed by *Howard Jacobsen* of *Triad*, Fairfax, California.

The typefaces are ITC Garamond Light and ITC Franklin Gothic Demi, set at *Type by Design*, Fairfax.

Production assistants were *Michael Fennelly* (design),

Sara Schrom (typography), and *Mark Shepard* (mechanical production).

Color separations, halftones, printing, and binding were executed by

Dai Nippon Printing Co., Ltd., Tokyo, Japan.

· North Fork of the Yuba River ·